SUCCESSFUL GARDENING WITHOUT SOIL

SUCCESSFUL GARDENING WITHOUT SOIL

by

C. E. TICQUET

Hon. Sec. Soilless Culture Society

With a Foreword by
PROFESSOR R. H. STOUGHTON, D.Sc.

1956
CHEMICAL PUBLISHING Co., Inc.
212 FIFTH AVENUE   NEW YORK, N.Y.

First American Edition
1956
CHEMICAL PUBLISHING Co., INC.
212 Fifth Avenue   New York, N.Y.

Printed in the United States of America

CONTENTS

		PAGE
	FOREWORD by Professor R. H. Stoughton, D.Sc.	7
	PREFACE	8

CHAPTER

1.	THE BEGINNINGS	9
2.	WATER	12
3.	THEORY OF SOLUTIONS	16
4.	THE SOLUTION IN PRACTICE	22
5.	MAKING AND MIXING	35
6.	MANAGEMENT OF SOLUTIONS	42
7.	WATER CULTURE	55
8.	SAND CULTURE	73
9.	GRAVEL CULTURE	98
10.	COMMERCIAL SOILLESS CULTURE	122
11.	SOILLESS CULTURE FOR EDUCATION	138
12.	WHERE HAVE I GONE WRONG?	150
13.	THE FUTURE	160
	APPENDIX	165
	BIBLIOGRAPHY	174

LIST OF ILLUSTRATIONS

(*Between pages 72 and 73*)

1. Growing lettuces by sub-irrigation.
2. Glass wool on gravel beds.
3. The author tending one of his crops of tomatoes.
4. A prize-winning truss of tomatoes.
5. Experimental bed covering for carnations.
6. Young cucumbers growing in a gravel bed.
7. Oil drum containing solution to irrigate a small gravel bed.
8. Soilless culture beds in a Yorkshire green-house.
9. The end of a good crop in gravel.
10. A truss of Stonor's Exhibition tomatoes.
11. Metal growing beds, feed tank, pipes and valves.
12. Young tomato plants in pots of sand.
13. The drip feed.
14. Root development in sand.
15. Fish aquarium converted to grow tomatoes by water culture.
16. A typical hobby outfit for sub-irrigation.
17. A larger growing tray.
18. A window-box soilless culture unit.
19. Mr. S. R. Mullard, the soilless culture pioneer, examines a lettuce root.
20. An armful of first quality sand-grown carnations.
21. Cauliflowers seven weeks after planting out in Calcutta.

FOREWORD

By Professor R. H. STOUGHTON, D.SC.

THE idea of the application of the sand- and water-culture methods of plant physiologists to the practical growing of plants by the amateur and the commercial grower has passed through the stages of incredulity, enthusiasm, derision, scepticism, and finally to sober acceptance, since the first proposals of Dr. F. Gericke in 1936. What was for long a stunt has become almost a commonplace in a surprisingly short time, so that now there is nothing remarkable in hearing that a grower with some acres of glass has turned over wholly or mainly to nutrient solution cultivation in sand or gravel.

This is not to say, however, that there is not still much to be learnt in this new application of scientific method. Unexpected, or at least unforeseen, difficulties and even disasters occur, all the worse in that if anything does go wrong all the plants under the same treatment are likely to be affected, instead of, as in soil, perhaps only a few in one bed. But with increasing experience and research these troubles can be guarded against or sometimes overcome after they have started, though in this as with all gardening matters, prevention is far better than cure.

Let no one fall into the trap of thinking that these methods are foolproof or even easier than the age-old ways of growing in soil. It must always be remembered that the plant itself is still the same; knowledge of its habits, its needs for particular light and temperature conditions, the pests and the diseases which may attack it, in short, its management, is no less necessary than before. After all, soilless cultivation is but an attempt to achieve one more step towards the goal of all good gardeners and plant research workers, control over the conditions under which the plant grows, its environment, to the betterment of man's profit or aesthetic enjoyment.

Although, therefore, to attain success with solution culture one must have at least as much knowledge and experience of the growing of the particular plant as ever, yet much of the factual aspect of the systems, the "know-how," can be acquired from books. The author of this book, himself an enthusiastic practitioner of soilless cultivation, has put down from his own experience and that of others a clear account of the principles and practice of the methods, which will start the feet of the beginner on the right path and save him from many pitfalls. Though an enthusiast, he does not allow his fervour to cloud his judgment and he courageously draws attention to the views of some of the decriers before he begins his own instructions.

Not only the beginner but the established grower also will find much of interest and guidance in these pages, set out with clarity and simplicity so that one need not be a chemist to understand the making-up of solutions or a plant physiologist to learn something of deficiency disorders, though one must still and ever be a gardener. However great may be advances in scientific knowledge of chemical testing, temperature control, light and moisture requirements and so on, yet the plant itself remains a living organism which can tell its own tale to the initiated better than any instrument.

PREFACE

IN the days when nurserymen were not as scrupulous as they are today, the best produce was sometimes found on top of the basket and the worst below. The indignant buyer then formed an immediate opinion of the seller, and went off to try someone else.

Something of the same sort seems to be in danger of happening with soilless culture. With more enthusiasm than wisdom, a number of writers have emphasised the advantages and glossed over the difficulties. Keen gardeners have been led to take up the new method of growth without being warned of the pitfalls. In contrast with the few who have persisted and won through, many have given the whole thing up in despair.

This is unfortunate. Soilless culture *has* real advantages. It *does* work—and work well, provided it is done properly. But the newcomer must realise at the outset that it is more difficult to produce results than with soil. There are many more factors which may go wrong.

So before you begin this book, I warn you I have turned the basket upside down and shown you the worst first. I have tried never to gloss over a difficulty or drawback.

But if, realising these limitations, you go on, you will find many unexpected rewards—including the thrill of achieving Nature's purpose in a way that only those who live in this modern age can know.

C. E. T.

1

THE BEGINNINGS

THE Americans are the biggest exponents of soilless culture today. But everybody seems agreed that it was an Englishman, John Woodward, who started growing plants without soil. In 1699 he cultivated them in various kinds of water to which he added garden soil. His most celebrated experiment was with spearmint. With this he managed to prove that it was earth and not water that made plants grow.

It was more than a hundred years before the subject was systematically studied again. Then a Frenchman, De Saussure, put forward in 1804 the idea that plants were made up of elements extracted from water, soil, and air.

Another Frenchman, chemist Jean Boussingault, found that the carbon and oxygen in growing tissues came from the air, and the hydrogen from water. The fact that nitrogen was contained in plants was also discovered by him.

Sachs and Knop, however, were the real pioneers of nutrient solutions as we understand them today. They germinated seeds on muslin tied over small jars, feeding the roots with chemical solutions. Those same methods, with a few improvements, are used in botanical laboratories today.

The seed-and-jar method showed that, to grow properly, a plant solution must contain nitrogen, potassium, phosphorous, magnesium, calcium, and sulphur.

Those six elements are now called the major elements, or if you want to be a little more technical, macro-nutrients.

Later it was discovered that in addition to the six macro-nutrients, iron was vital to growth. Then manganese, boron, copper, zinc, and—quite recently—molybdenum were all found to be essential. As only very small amounts—or traces—of these elements were needed, they were called the trace, or minor, elements. Another term used is micro-nutrients.

Many of these elements are always present even in pure chemicals, so it was a long and complicated process to prove that plants died without them. In some cases a single seed contained enough to last a plant for more than one generation. But, proved it was, and today we use the knowledge gained by the patience of our predecessors.

Nor is the end anywhere in sight. If they can only devise methods exact enough, the scientists will probably be able to prove sooner or later that uranium (of atom fame), vanadium, selenium, and a host of other obscure elements found in plant tissue are there for a purpose, and not by chance. Already aluminium, silicon, chlorine, and gallium are *almost* on the "essential" list.

Fortunately for those who just want to grow a few plants without soil—and without too much trouble—there are enough of all these "iums" in the fertiliser-grade salts usually used. So having mentioned them, we can forget them.

Not until the early 1920's did it occur to anyone that amateur and commercial crop production might be feasible without soil.

It was Dr. W. F. Gericke of California who in 1929 took the great step of bringing water culture out of the laboratory into the greenhouse and garden.

The results of the Gericke system were remarkable.

The Press took up the theme—with variations. Amateur enthusiasts got busy all over America, and in Europe, too. Misguided experimenters (myself included) threw a handful of chemicals into a jar or tin, filled up from the kitchen tap, and sat back to watch the "miracle". Of course, nothing happened.

What went wrong? Nothing, really. Dr. Gericke *did* get astonishing results—but under a Californian sun. His tomatoes *did* require a ladder to pick them—but with warm solution, and under the guidance of a super-expert.

Hard on the heels of water culture, but without all the publicity, came sand culture. This was easier, and cheaper, and altogether more understandable to the grower who had been used to soil. But it had its drawbacks. The labour of watering was one.

Labour-saving was the thought behind the introduction of beds of gravel or cinders fed automatically by solution pumps. This was eminently suited to operations on a big scale, and when difficulties of providing troops scattered in tropic outposts with fresh vegetables led the United States Air Force to take up soilless culture to save shipping space, it was this system that was used. In 1945 the first big installation was laid down on Ascension Island. Then the world's biggest installation of some eighty acres was put into operation in Japan.

Since the war a new system of feeding beds by solution flowing along channels, or flumes, has been evolved. It is cheaper to instal than piping, and is becoming steadily more popular.

Which brings our rather sketchy history up to the present day.

2

WATER

THERE are three ways of growing plants without soil:

1. Water culture, usually known as hydroponics.
2. Sand culture.
3. Sub-irrigation, in which gravel, cinders, pumice, or several other materials consisting of small solid particles may be used.

The one thing common to all these is water. Yet it is the water which the average would-be grower forgets. Drinkable water is well-nigh universal in the British Isles, and so we hardly ever give it a thought. Yet it is a fact that there is almost as much difference between some samples of water and others as there is between chalk and cheese. These differences may be important to anyone using the water for soilless culture.

So I advise you, if you are only doing things in a small way in the greenhouse or on the front-room window-ledge, to use rain water. It is easy to collect, by putting a barrel or old tank under a gutter-spout. If you have a greenhouse you probably collect it for watering the plants in any case.

If you are doing things on a bigger scale, and have to use water from the mains or from a well or stream, then there is only one safe thing to do—find out what the supply contains.

WATER

Our water system is looked after by a series of undertakings who draw from hills or rivers all over the country. Sometimes it is a corporation or council, sometimes a water board or similar body. What you have to do is to find out who actually supplies the water you use, and then write to the engineer or analyst concerned. They have to make regular analyses in the ordinary course of events, and are usually quite happy to tell you what they are.

Here is a typical one, in this case for the City of Birmingham:

Calcium	0·5
Sodium	0·5
Magnesium	0·2
Potassium	0·1
Iron	0·1
Bicarbonate	1·3
Chlorine	0·8
Sulphate	0·6
Silicate	0·3
Undetermined	0·1
	4·5 parts per 100,000

Soilless culture solutions are usually worked out in parts per million cubic centimetres, so if we multiply those figures by ten we get the right amounts for our calculations.

Four of the elements given above are directly concerned in our solutions—calcium, magnesium, potassium, and iron. Let us take one example to show how the analysis affects us. Suppose we are using a solution containing 150 p.p.m. of potassium. The above figures show that there is only one ($0·1 \times 10$) part per million present in the water. Obviously, therefore, we can proceed happily in the knowledge that there is nothing in the water to affect our calculations.

The Birmingham water, as a matter of fact, is unusually pure—it is almost equal to distilled water. Some supplies are very different. Occasionally they may contain enough calcium to supply half what we need.

Fylde Water Board, for example, which supplies parts of Lancashire, contains three times the amount of calcium that is in the Midland supply. Here is an abbreviated analysis:

	Parts per million
Total solids	76·8
Total calcium as *Ca*	15·4
Chlorides	9·5
Silica	3·5

The golden rule is this. If the amount of any element is more than 20 per cent. of the total of that element you want in your solution, take it into account in working out the weight of chemical to add. Otherwise you can ignore it.

In practice this means that if the amounts in your water are less than the following, you need not bother about them:

	Parts per million
Phosphorous, Magnesium	10
Nitrogen, Potassium	25
Calcium, Sulphate	40
Iron	1
Other trace elements	0·2

Calcium and magnesium are usually the only elements which may have to be taken into account, though sometimes iron is found in appreciable amounts as well. Occasionally, if there is an epidemic and the water supply has been chlorinated more than usual for medical reasons, it may be present in sufficient quantity to affect plant growth.

Actually the Fylde supply quoted above is as near the damage level for chlorine as is desirable. Amounts of more than ten parts per million are suspect. Free chlorine can be removed by letting the water stand in the open air for several hours.

Heavy metals, such as copper and zinc, can be got out of water by allowing it to flow through a deep bed of calcareous sand. But this is tedious, and I hope you are not unlucky enough to have to do it.

Of course, if you are using a ready-made-up nutrient tablet, you will not be able to adjust it to allow for any nutrient chemical in the water. But such tablets are quite satisfactory for hobby purposes, and as they are usually used with small installations, sufficient rain water can be assumed to be available.

3

THEORY OF SOLUTIONS

Most people, especially those new to soilless culture, regard the formula for the solution as the secret of the whole business. Actually it is only one factor, and not always the most important one at that.

So much has been talked and written about formulæ—particularly by people with a commercial interest in view—that they have been invested with an air of mystery which is quite unjustified.

The truth is that there are many different solutions which will grow plants satisfactorily, and the chemicals in the solutions can range over quite large amounts without much difference in the result. Theoretically there is a best solution for each different crop and each different stage of it. There is even a theoretical best solution for each part of the world and each phase of the climate in it.

But if you tried to adjust your solution to such fine limits you would be attempting the impossible. My advice is to start with only one formula, vary it quite simply in the way described later in this chapter, and leave it at that. Later, when you feel more confident, you can mix as many different solutions as you like. But at first YOU are the one likely to get mixed.

Now to consider the formula we ought to use. Proper handling of soilless culture solutions is difficult enough as it is, so let us be as simple as we can, with no more complications than we can help. First of all, what *is* a nutrient solution?

It is a solution of chemicals in water, so compounded that it contains all the six major elements and the minor elements as well. In case you skipped Chapter One, that means the following:

Major Elements	*Minor Elements*
Nitrogen	Iron
Potassium	Manganese
Phosphorus	Boron
Magnesium	Copper
Calcium	Zinc
Sulphur	Molybdenum

Of these, we can afford to ignore molybdenum altogether, and unless we have definite evidence of a shortage, usually copper and zinc as well.

The other elements are all vital. In whatever way you make up your solution, they must figure in it.

This does not mean that there is one successful combination of salts and no other. When you go into the subject, it is astounding how big are the differences between solutions reported as successfully used in different parts of the world. Here are a few for tomatoes, just for comparison:

ELEMENTS IN PARTS PER MILLION

	Nitrogen	Potassium	Phosphorous	Magnesium	Calcium
Reading University	300	150	70	50	400
Leeds University	110	145	37	—	95
Godber Nursery Cornwall	130	120	60	58	290
Foxwell's Nursery, Sussex	92	254	52	50	310

Here are two formulæ for carnations:

	N.	K.	P.	Mg.	Ca.
J. W. Sparkes' Nursery, Sussex	350	100	100	20	—
A Lancashire Nursery	120	100	65	50	—

These are all formulæ which have been used in England. Of course they are not used all the year round, and they are not necessarily the formulæ now employed by the growers named.

Even greater differences are noted in comparison with the mixtures used abroad:

	N.	K.	P.	Mg.	Ca.
U.S. Army "B"	168	390	63	96	200
Ohio "WP"	113	250	65	51	310
Purdue "2D"	170	395	31	120	200
New Jersey	230	170	130	58	280
Gericke (California)	168	390	63	24	80

Now one of the advantages of soilless culture is that it is controlled growth—you can give your plants more or less what you want them to have in the way of nourishment, instead of what happens to be in your soil.

How, then, can we reconcile all these different formulæ? Wouldn't it be just as easy, and almost as likely to be successful, if we just dropped a few spoonfuls of salts into the water and hoped for the best?

Not quite. Let us look at these formulæ in a little more detail. Take first, the calcium. With two exceptions, all the figures are between 200 and 400. Calcium, as it happens, is available for use in normal fertiliser form only in fairly insoluble salts, and it is doubtful whether, even though a particular formula specifies a certain figure for calcium, it is really all in solution. So that when one grower uses half as much calcium again as another, it is as likely as not that the amount available *to the plant* is not very different. Comparatively large differences in calcium, therefore, need not mean a great deal.

Next, magnesium. With exceptions of Gericke and Sparkes, everyone apparently believes that the right amount is over fifty parts per million.

And what about the people who recommend larger amounts? The answer, apparently, is that magnesium is an element that does no great harm if it is present to excess. It is a deficiency of it that matters. So that there is no real disagreement here. Provided you are at the over-fifty mark, all is well.

Phosphorus seems to be responsible for the least difference of opinion of all. With the inevitable exceptions, somewhere about sixty parts per million seems to be the agreed figure in most parts of the world.

It is in the nitrogen and potassium columns that everybody seems to have a different idea. And the reason is that it is by varying the amounts of these two elements that the soilless culturist adapts his solution to the season and to the plant.

If you were to draw a graph from the nitrogen and potassium figures above, which are taken quite at random from the 200 or so formulæ reported as used in various places, you would get something like the diagram on the next page.

Each dot represents one formula, fixed by reading the amount of nitrogen up the vertical line, and the amount of potassium along the other line.

Now the really vital point to note about the graph is this: THE DOTS ARE GROUPED ALONG TWO DISTINCT LINES.

In the graph the lines are shown one dotted and one wavy. The dotted line is drawn so that any point on it shows twice as much potassium as nitrogen, and the wavy line so that any point reads twice as much nitrogen as potassium.

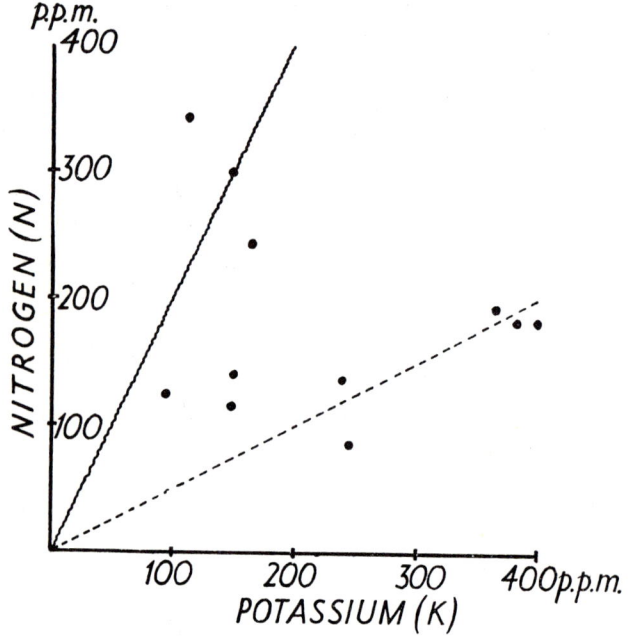

The lower, dotted, line is the ratio used in winter, and the, upper, wavy line is the ratio used in summer. This simple ratio, called the nitrogen-potassium balance, is the real secret of nutrient solution formulæ, if secret there is at all.

Nearly every successful formula which I have encountered in use in this country approximates more or less to this definition: In summer it allows up to twice as much N as K; and in winter up to twice as much K as N.

The other elements, once a suitable figure has been decided upon, remain unaltered unless other factors have to be considered, as in the case of phosphorous, which is dealt with in the Section on sand culture.

The other fundamental factor is this: the actual amounts of elements are not so important as the ratio between them. You can, for example, halve the quantities of all your salts, or even double them, without a great deal of harm. But if you halve or double the amount, say, of phosphorous alone, you throw the whole solution out of balance and trouble results. This doubling or halving the concentrations is in fact sometimes done deliberately for special purposes, as explained in the chapter on management of solutions.

So much, then, for the theory of formulæ. How can we translate it into practice? Here, I suggest, is the basic formula which is most suitable for growth under average conditions:

Nitrogen	*Potassium*	*Phosphorous*	*Magnesium*	*Calcium*
200	200	60	50	300

The nitrogen and potassium, of course, represent only average values. In the middle of winter or the height of summer they will vary in the ratio explained above. But in general, and bearing in mind the usual British climatic conditions and the type of crops usually grown, the figures represent the happy medium for our type of growth.

4

THE SOLUTION IN PRACTICE

WE have decided on the best formula on which to work as a basis. How do we make it up?

The particular form in which the elements are provided is not absolutely vital. Nitrogen, for example, can be given as sodium nitrate, potassium nitrate, calcium nitrate, or even in one of the ammonium salts.

Whichever salt is used, the calculation of the total amount of the element being provided is most easily understood in what is known as the "parts per million" form. That means parts per million cubic centimetres of water. Since the French obligingly made the weight of a c.c. of water one gram, we can equally well say grams per million grams of water, or grams per million cubic centimetres.

So when we describe a solution as containing 200 p.p.m. of nitrogen, we mean 200 grams of nitrogen per million cubic centimetres of water.

All chemical salts consist of elements combined together. Potassium nitrate, for example, combines potassium, nitrogen, and oxygen in the formula KNO_3.

Each of these elements has its own atomic weight, potassium is 39, nitrogen 14 and oxygen 16. So the atomic weights of this particular salt are:

$$K \quad N \quad O$$
$$39 + 14 + [(16 \times 3) = 48]$$

which totals 101.

THE SOLUTION IN PRACTICE

Each 101 grams of potassium nitrate, therefore, contain 14 grams of nitrogen. If then, we were aiming at a solution containing one part per million of nitrogen (or one gram per million c.c.), we need:

$\frac{101}{14}$ grams of potassium nitrate in a million cubic centimetres of water. And for 200 p.p.m., it is:

$$\frac{101}{14} \times 200 = 1{,}443 \text{ grams.}$$

In actual use, however, nearly all the fertiliser grades of salts used for growing purposes contain impurities which add to the weight without adding to the amount of the element we need. In the case of potassium nitrate, these impurities add about 9 grams to the total. Adding that weight to 101, therefore, we learn that 110 grams of the salt contain 14 grams of nitrogen. Our final calculation, it turns out, would thus be:

$$\frac{110}{14} \times 200 = \frac{22{,}000}{14} = 1{,}571 \text{ grams.}$$

The same method is used in working out the amount of any element. All that must be known is the total of atomic weights, or molecular weight, as it is called, and the amount of impurities. A list of the "impurity weights" of the more common salts is given at the end of this book. In the case of those not given, inquiry must be made of the suppliers.

The quantity worked out, as we stated at the outset, is for 1,000,000 c.c., or 1,000 litres. The average person prefers to work in ounces per gallon or some multiple of gallons. Let us suppose, therefore, that we are requiring 200 p.p.m. N in 100 gallons of water.

We know by the above calculation that for this concentration we need 1,571 grams per 1,000 litres. The amount for one litre is therefore:

$$\frac{1,571}{1,000} = 1\cdot 571 \text{ grams.}$$

By a table you will find in any good ready reckoner, if we multiply grams per litre by $1\cdot 6$, we arrive at ounces per 10 gallons.

The number of ounces required for 10 gallons is, therefore:

$$1\cdot 571 \times 1\cdot 6$$

and for 100 gallons:

$$1\cdot 571 \times 1\cdot 6 \times 10$$
$$= 1\cdot 571 \times 16$$
$$= 25\cdot 136$$
$$= 25 \text{ ozs. approx.}$$

In the appendix to this book will be found a guide to the preparation of nutrient solutions. If the amount of potassium nitrate required is worked out by reference to this table, the actual amount for 200 p.p.m. in 100 gallons is found to be 24·4 oz. The difference of 0·6 oz. is accounted for by the different sources of supply of the salt, and is negligible. Unless the composition of the salt is known to be radically different from normal, the table in the appendix can be taken as a good guide for general purposes. If it is desired to be especially accurate, or if a salt is being used which does not appear in the table, then it will be necessary to work out the amount in accordance with the method detailed above.

Now our formula is to be:

N.	K.	P.	Mg.	Ca.
200	200	60	50	300

So far we have 200 p.p.m. N in the 25 oz. of potassium nitrate. But this salt also supplies potassium.

Referring to the appendix table again, we find that the weight of potassium nitrate which gives one part per million of nitrogen also gives 2·8 p.p.m. of potassium. If, therefore, we have 200 p.p.m. N, we have:

$$200 \times 2\cdot80 = 560 \text{ p.p.m. } K.$$

But our formula calls for 200 p.p.m. K. So we have nearly three times the amount required. This, of course, is patently absurd. I have included the calculation only because it pin-points one of the commonest errors made in calculating, and stresses the rule: *always calculate first the element of which the salt contains most.*

Retracing a little, then, we need to find FIRST the amount of potassium nitrate which gives in 100 gallons of water the concentration 200 p.p.m. K. By the table, this is:

$$0\cdot044 \times 200 = 8\cdot8 \text{ oz.}$$
$$= 8\tfrac{3}{4} \text{ oz. approx.}$$

And this amount also gives $200 \times 0\cdot36\ N = 72\ N$.

Now we must find the extra 128 p.p.m. N required. We can give it with sodium nitrate or ammonium sulphate. Experience, however, shows that the use of more than one-third of the total nitrogen as ammonium nitrogen leads to trouble because of rapid assimilation. Suppose, therefore, we give 100 p.p.m. from sodium nitrate and 28 p.p.m. from ammonium sulphate.

For the remaining nitrogen, then, we need sodium nitrate $0\cdot103 \times 100 = 10\cdot3$ ounces = $10\tfrac{1}{4}$ oz. approx. ammonium sulphate $0\cdot076 \times 28 = 2$ ounces approx.

So far then, we have 200 p.p.m. N and 200 p.p.m. K.

Similarly for 60 P we need:

Monocalcium phosphate $0.118 \times 60 = 7$ oz. approx.

And this also gives 0.6×60 p.p.m. $Ca = 36$ p.p.m. Ca.

To find the required 300 p.p.m. Ca, we need another 264 p.p.m. Using gypsum, this works out at:

$$0.076 \times 264 = 20.06 = 20 \text{ oz. approx.}$$

Finally for Mg, we need:

$0.172 \times 50 = 8.6 = 8\frac{1}{2}$ oz. approx. magnesium sulphate.

Our final formula for the major elements therefore for 100 gallons is:

Potassium nitrate	$8\frac{3}{4}$ oz.
Sodium nitrate	$10\frac{1}{4}$ oz.
Ammonium sulphate	2 oz.
Monocalcium phosphate	7 oz.
Magnesium sulphate	$8\frac{1}{2}$ oz.
Calcium sulphate	$13\frac{3}{4}$ oz.

We still need, however, our trace elements—iron, manganese, and boron. Copper and zinc we need not bother with unless they are proved necessary.

Most of the British growers or research workers who have published their formulæ recommend the following amounts:

Iron	5 p.p.m.
Manganese	1 p.p.m.
Boron	1 p.p.m.
Copper and Zinc	0.5 p.p.m.

THE SOLUTION IN PRACTICE

My own experience indicates that it is not necessary to use anything like these amounts. In my view the following amounts are quite sufficient:

> Iron   3   p.p.m.
> Manganese   0·5 p.p.m.
> Boron   0·5 p.p.m.
> Copper and Zinc Not added unless experience indicates otherwise.

Reverting once more to the table at the end of the book, we find that this works out at:

> Ferrous sulphate   0·089 × 3   = 0·267 oz.
> Manganese sulphate   0·065 × 0·5 = 0·03 oz.
> Boric acid   0·090 × 0·5 = 0·04 oz.

It is manifestly out of the question to weigh such small amounts out in ounces. So what we do is to make a much stronger concentration, and then dilute it down for use. The amounts above, it will be remembered are for 100 gallons. This is the basic amount of solution we decided to make up at one time. If, then, we multiply the amounts ten times, we shall have enough trace solution for ten lots of the main solution.

The amounts then work out at:

> Iron sulphate   2·67 = 2½ oz. approx.
> Manganese sulphate   0·3 = One-third oz.
> Boric acid   0·4 = Two-fifths oz.

But it is still obviously not very practical to keep 100 gallons of trace element solution. So if we dissolve the above amounts in, say, *one* gallon, we shall get a more manageable amount, which can be conveniently kept in a large bottle. But this gallon still contains sufficient salts for ten applications of trace elements. Expressed another way, if we add one-tenth of a gallon, or 16 fluid ounces, to each 100 gallons of major element solution, we shall be in order. This is in fact the right thing to do.

In order to prevent precipitation of the iron during storage, acid is added to the concentrate. A suitable amount is 2·5 c.c. per gallon of concentrated sulphuric acid. *CAUTION:* The acid must always be added to the water, slowly, *not* water to the acid.

There is another, and, in some ways, simpler method of calculating solutions, which is based on the percentage of the element required.

Suppose, for example, we need to make up a solution containing 200 p.p.m. of nitrogen. We have decided to use calcium nitrate. The molecular weight for this salt, allowing for impurities is 180, and each 180 grams will therefore contain 28 grams (2×14) of nitrogen. This is arrived at from the formula $Ca(NO_3)_2$. The percentage of N is therefore:

$$\frac{28}{180} \times 100$$
$$= 15 \cdot 5 \%$$

The amount of calcium nitrate required therefore for one part per million is:

$$\frac{100}{\% \text{ element}} \times \frac{\text{Volume of solution in c.c}}{1,000,000}$$

which equals:

$$\frac{\text{litres of solution}}{10 \text{ times } \% \text{ element}}$$

In the case of calcium nitrate, the amount for one part per million of N. for say 1,000 litres is, therefore:

$$\frac{1,000}{10 \times 15\cdot 5} = \frac{100}{15\cdot 5} = 6\cdot 45 \text{ grams.}$$

and for 200 p.p.m.:

$$6\cdot 45 \times 200 = 1290 \text{ grams.}$$

The amounts then have to be adjusted for gallons and pounds and ounces. If a list of percentages is compiled this is a quicker method of working out than with molecular weights. Once the volume of solution is known, a list of weights can be kept which give one part per million in that volume. To work out the amount for each required part per million is then a matter of a moment.

The salts selected for the examples in making up a solution are not, of course the only ones that can be used. Almost any chemical that will give the required elements may be used. In practice the governing considerations are:

1. Solubility.
2. Availability.
3. Cost.
4. Convenience, which includes the stipulation that the salts must keep fairly well without special methods of storage.

Bearing in mind these factors, there is really no need to consider more than these chemicals: potassium nitrate, calcium nitrate, sodium nitrate, ammonium sulphate, potassium sulphate, potassium chloride, monocalcium phosphate, superphosphate, magnesium sulphate, mono-ammonium phosphate, calcium sulphate (plaster of Paris) and calcium sulphate (gypsum).

Considering these in order:

NITROGEN SALTS

Potassium nitrate is the most generally useful of all the salts. It is easily available, keeps well, and is very soluble.

Calcium nitrate is expensive, and unless bought as the concentrated solution it is difficult to keep without absorbing moisture. It is, however, very useful when both calcium and nitrogen are required but not potassium.

Sodium nitrate is cheap, very soluble, and stores well if kept fairly air-tight. It is indispensable when nitrogen only is required. Used in large amounts, however, it may cause complications because of the large additions of sodium.

Ammonium sulphate is cheap, easy to get, and easy to keep. It is invaluable for adding easily—assimilable nitrogen, but used in too great a proportion is apt to cause soft sappy growth.

POTASSIUM SALTS

Potassium sulphate, easily obtained except in wartime, is indispensable for adding potassium alone. It stores well. Like potassium chloride, it is very soluble.

Potassium chloride is an alternative to potassium sulphate, but it is not so desirable because of the risk of chlorine injury.

MAGNESIUM SALTS

Magnesium sulphate, more popularly known as Epsom Salts, is practically the only salt used in normal practice. It is common, cheap, dissolves very easily and keeps well. There is another grade, called anhydrous magnesium sulphate, but this is more difficult to get and offers no advantage in use except that less of it is required. The Epsom Salt grade is almost half water due to the water of crystallisation.

PHOSPHOROUS SALTS

More confusion exists regarding the phosphorous salts than with all the other salts combined. There are only three possible salts to use, but there are so many forms of them that it is not always easy to know exactly with what one has to deal. The salts are the phosphates of ammonia, calcium and potassium.

Ammonium salts are relatively simple. They are:

	% *Phosphorous* (P)
Ammonium phosphate (food grade)	26
Ammonium phosphate (fertiliser grade)	21

Both these are useful when the amount of nitrogen is not critical, and when it is desired to add phosphorous without adding calcium. They are, however, too expensive for commercial use.

The calcium salts are:

	%P.
Monocalcium phosphate (food grade)	24
Monocalcium phosphate (treble superphosphate)	21
Monocalcium phosphate (common superphosphate)	8

All these have the formula $Ca\ H_4(PO_4)_2$, but they differ in the amount of impurities. In the first two it is largely water of crystallisation, and in the case of the superphosphate chiefly calcium sulphate.

The best to use is undoubtedly the middle one—the treble superphosphate. It is reasonably cheap, and contains a useful percentage of phosphorous. Unfortunately, it is not easily obtainable in the British Isles, and growers are often forced back on the superphosphate, which is much cheaper and easier to obtain. Superphosphate may on occasion even be more desirable, since it supplies in addition calcium sulphate and quite possibly trace elements too.

The food grade of monocalcium phosphate is fairly easily obtainable from the wholesale chemists or even the retail druggists, but is expensive.

The complications arise chiefly from the different names in use for the same salt. If you go into a retail chemist and simply ask for calcium phosphate, you will get the insoluble salt calcium ortho-phosphate, with the formula $Ca_3(PO_4)_2$, also known, chiefly in the United States, as tricalcium phosphate. The Americans have another habit of calling what we know as calcium dihydrogen phosphate dicalcium orthophosphate.

The chemical manufacturers, on the other hand, sell what they call monobasic calcium phosphate or acid calcium phosphate which is simply our old friend monocalcium phosphate (food grade) in disguise.

A further complication is that some makers supply what is called monocalcium phosphate (food grade) but which as far as I have been able to find out is actually equivalent to treble superphosphate in the amount of phosphorous contained.

The only safe way is to ask the supplier to specify the

amount of P_2O_5, from which the amount of P can, of course, be easily worked out in the ratio $\frac{31}{71}$.

The other remaining phosphorous salt is monopotassium phosphate (KH_2PO_4), which is quite straightforward.

All phosphorous salts keep well.

CALCIUM SALTS

Apart from calcium nitrate, which has already been dealt with, the only two practicable choices are:
Calcium sulphate (gypsum), and
Calcium sulphate (plaster of Paris).

The latter contains 21 per cent. of calcium, which is more than the gypsum, but it is dearer. It dissolves more easily, however, and in my view is the better of the two.

Calcium chloride is sometimes used, but is not really necessary with all the other combinations.

The calcium salts keep with less trouble than any. They are, however, the hardest to dissolve.

Trace element salts offer a more restricted choice than with the major elements. The following are usually used:

IRON SALTS

Ferrous sulphate	$FeSO_4\, 7\, H_2O$
Ferric chloride	$FeCl_3\, 6\, H_2O$
Ferric ammonium citrate	$Fe(NH_4)_3(C_6H_5O_7)_2$

Of these the commonest and cheapest is ferrous sulphate. It does not stay in solution so well as ferric ammonium citrate, however, and for this reason is less desirable. The ammonium citrate salt is also the better to use when the solution tends to be alkaline.

MANGANESE SALTS

Manganese sulphate $MnSO_4\ 4H_2O$
Manganese chloride $MnCl_2\ 4H_2O$

Manganese sulphate is the more common salt. It should be kept in an air-tight bottle.

BORON

Boric Acid H_3BO_3
Borax $Na_2B_4O_7\ 10H_2O$

Boric acid is the better of the two for the supply of boron. It mixes more satisfactorily with the other trace elements when a complete trace element solution is required.

If the other trace elements are wanted, there is no need to look further than copper sulphate ($CuSO_4\ 5H_2O$) and zinc sulphate ($ZnSO_4 7\ H_2O$).

One other chemical is quite often encountered in soilless culture practice—ammonium nitrate. It frequently causes too-rapid assimilation of nitrogen, however, and is best avoided for that reason.

All chemicals are best stored in large stoppered jars or asphalted tins, fitted with lids. In large quantities, wooden boxes are quite suitable. They should be raised off the floor. As certain salts give off slightly corrosive fumes, metal tools should not be kept near them.

5

MAKING AND MIXING

THE first essential to weighing is something to weigh with. Yet it is surprising how many growers borrow the first pair of broken-down scales that come to hand in the fond hope that they will weigh somewhere near the amounts they require. I have visited smart expertly-run nurseries and then on entering the chemical room have been appalled at a rusty, corroded pair of scales that must have been rescued from some junk-heap.

I have even known gardener husbands borrow their wives' kitchen scales. This may be more accurate, but it is liable to lead to trouble of another sort, especially if the cook mistakes the white powder left on the pan for flour!

A pair of second-hand fruiterer's scales or the like will do as a temporary make-shift, but if good work is to be done there is really no alternative but to obtain some laboratory scales. A pair weighing up to four pounds is quite big enough, and can be obtained new, complete with weights, for less than five pounds. Either gram or pound-ounce weights may be used. These scales will be accurate to one gram, and will include a non-corrodible pan. The centre indicator arm will enable weighing to be done with a knowledge that the amounts intended will be correct.

For putting the chemicals on to the scales there is nothing better than a large wooden or bone spoon. No need to be afraid of raiding the kitchen here!

After each weighing, the scales pan should be wiped to prevent particles of chemical adhering and causing stains.

When mixing, I have found nothing better for dissolving chemicals in than an enamel bucket. Each quantity of salt can be first thrown into the bucket, previously filled with water (preferably hot), stirred and mixed, and then transferred to the tank containing the solution being made up.

At one time there seemed to be little point in the order in which the chemicals were added. Some people recommended dissolving the less soluble salts first, on the principle that they had more "elbow-room", so to speak. Others recommended the more soluble salts first. Later experience, however, shows that there is a definite order in which the salts should be added in order to prevent risk of inter-reaction throwing the solution out of balance. This order is as follows:

1. Magnesium sulphate.

2. Monocalcium phosphate.

3. Potassium nitrate, or calcium nitrate, or potassium chloride, or potassium sulphate, or sodium nitrate.

If more than one of these chemicals is used, they should be added in the given order. For example, calcium nitrate before potassium sulphate.

4. Calcium sulphate.

Similarly, there is a definite order for adding the minor elements, unless a complete minor element solution is added at one time. This order is:

1. Boric acid.
2. Zinc sulphate (if used).
3. Ferrous sulphate.
4. Manganese sulphate.
5. Copper sulphate (if used).

The object of this particular order is to avoid precipitation of some of the elements. For this reason, it is also wise to add the minor elements some hours before or after the major elements.

The minor elements for small quantities of solution have to be weighed on a chemical balance, as the amounts are so small that great accuracy is needed. For the average amateur without such a balance, a friendly druggist will usually oblige. The major element chemicals are weighed on the scales already described.

At least three-quarters of the quantity of solution to be made up should be present before any chemicals are added. For example, if 50 gallons of solution are to be mixed, 40 gallons of water should be run into the container before weighing begins. This ensures that there is sufficient water to dissolve all the chemicals easily. If the hot-water-bucket method is used, the additions of water from the bucket will make up most of the remaining amount. The hot water will also serve to take the chill off the solution and so tend to improve growth.

There will always be a certain amount of sediment at the bottom of the tank even when all the chemicals are dissolved. This consists of impurities, and in the case of superphosphate, of calcium sulphate, which only goes into solution very slowly. In addition, even with the covered type of container, dirt always finds its way into the solution and to the bottom. For this reason it is wise to swill the tank out every few months or so, so as to clear out this accumulation.

If the water to be used is considerably acid or alkaline (usually the latter) it should be adjusted to pH 7 before the addition of chemicals. The way to do this is described in the chapter on the management of solutions.

Weighing out the salts separately and stirring them one by one into the tank is the usual and the safest method. There are, however, two other ways which are each more convenient in their own particular sphere.

The first is the stock solution method. The principle of this has already been indicated in the method of adding trace elements and iron. It is to make concentrated solutions of each required chemical, and then add a measured quantity of liquid. Some salts, however, such as calcium sulphate, are comparatively low in solubility, and very concentrated solutions cannot be made.

The advantage of the system is that salts do not have to be weighed out afresh each time, and also that for small quantities of solution, the liquid method is both more convenient and more accurate.

As an example, take the case of potassium nitrate. Suppose that we are very modest in our experiments, and the total quantity of complete solution that we require is only five gallons. We need, let us say, 200 p.p.m. of potassium.

Now we know by the table in the appendix that for one part per million of potassium in 100 gallons we have to weigh 0·044 oz. of potassium nitrate. Therefore, for 200 p.p.m. we require:

$$0·044 \times 200 = 8·8 \text{ oz.}$$

but we are only making five gallons. Therefore, the amount needed is:

MAKING AND MIXING

$$\frac{8\cdot 8}{100} \times 5 \quad \text{(Since the amount in the table is for 100 gallons).}$$

This gives:

$$\frac{8\cdot 8}{20} = 0\cdot 44 \text{ oz.}$$

If, therefore, we weigh out 4·4 ounces of potassium nitrate, we have enough for ten times the amount of solution—that is for ten additions to each five-gallon quantity. A convenient amount of stock solution to store is one gallon. If, then, we dissolve 4·4 ounces in one gallon, we need to add one-tenth of one gallon of stock solution of potassium nitrate to each five gallons. A gallon contains 160 fluid ounces, so that we need to add 16 fluid ounces each time.

It will be obvious that this method is also convenient for changing the amount of potassium if desired. Suppose, for instance, that we decide to change to 150 p.p.m. K. We should then add:

$$\frac{16}{200} \times 150 \text{ fluid oz.}$$
which equals 12 fluid oz.

There are other methods of working out this stock solution method. Some people use what is called the molar system, in which the standard is the gram molecular weight (or mole) of the chemical dissolved in a litre of water. I have always found this confusing, however, and suggest that the ounce quantities calculation is much easier to understand.

The third method of mixing, the mixed dry salts method, is the most convenient of all for small amounts such as indoor vases and pots, but it is not possible to alter the composition of the solution once made. In this system all the chemicals are weighed out and thoroughly mixed together, a particular amount being weighed or measured out each time and added to a small quantity of water. The result is something like a "level teaspoonful per pint", which appeals to those who like the simplest form of instruction to follow.

Hygroscopic salts like calcium nitrate cannot be used, however, because the mixture cakes. Nor can any calcium salt be mixed with sodium nitrate. Formulæ for solutions which can be mixed dry are given at the end of this book.

This is the method of the dry mix:

All the chemicals required for a measured amount of solution are calculated, and then multiplied by some convenient number, such as ten, to allow for ten quantities to be made up. If the total, for instance, then comes to 30 oz., 3 oz. of mix are added each time. By experiment some suitable container, such as a large spoon, can be found which holds three ounces fairly accurately, and this can be used to get the required amount.

Two precautions to observe are that before weighing the chemicals are thoroughly powdered, and that after weighing they are thoroughly mixed together. In addition, the full amount of water needed should always be provided before any salt mixture is added.

Unless the solution amount is very large—thousands of gallons—it is not practicable to add minor elements by this method.

The mixed dry salts method is the basis of the several mixtures which are sold commercially for soilless culture. Some are marketed in pill form, some in powder form, and some in concentrated liquid form. Broadly speaking, however, they fall into three classes:

1. Those in which the composition is fixed. In these all the nutrients are contained in one packet or bottle.
2. Those in which the composition is partly adjustable. The usual method of achieving this is for several mixtures to be available, each having an application for a particular season or crop.
3. Those in which all the important elements are adjustable. The principle of this is that each pill contains one required element, and that the addition of more or less than the standard quantity alters the amount of that element.

Each of these products has its uses. The average gardener taking up soilless culture would probably find it convenient to begin with a fixed composition product such as Nutrigen and then progress through the other types as he gains confidence.

The amateur with the desire for only a novelty plant or two indoors might be content with the first or second stage.

Sooner or later, however, the grower who goes in for soilless culture in a bigger way, or who becomes so deeply interested as to wish to gain complete control of his solutions, graduates to the stage of making up and adjusting for himself. In this way he gains knowledge and confidence. It is also the most economical method of working on a bigger scale.

6

MANAGEMENT OF SOLUTIONS

Without a doubt the chief factor in the management of solutions is the correct achievement and adjustment of *pH*. It is difficult to emphasise this too much.

Visiting one big commercial grower in Devon, I enquired about the *pH*, and was told that it used to be checked, but that as the plants seemed to be doing quite well, he did not bother any more. I was not surprised to find that the plants did not seem to be doing well at all.

One reason for the neglect of the *pH* is that it is not always fully understood. Without going into the mysteries of the ionic theory, it should be realised that when the numbers of acid ions are equal to that of the alkaline ions, the reading on the *pH* scale is neutral, or *pH* 7. This is the reading for pure water. For every tenfold increase in the concentration of either the acid or the alkaline elements, the *pH* reading will go down or up one. *pH* 5, for example, is ten times as acid as *pH* 6. From this, it is obvious that if a solution is more acid or alkaline than recommended, it may be only one figure different in the scale, but it is ten times as different as far as the plant is concerned. If you ask for one more lump of sugar in your tea, you do not expect to get ten. If you do, it may sicken you. And that is exactly what happens to plants.

Plants—or some of them—*will* grow, after a fashion, at any *pH* between *pH* 4 and *pH* 8. But there is now enough experience of *pH* available to be able to state definitely that the best average is *pH* 5–*pH* 6·5, which is slightly acid. If you always aim at *pH* 6, you will not be far wrong.

Most satisfactory solutions do in fact make up at somewhere about the right *pH*. The difficulty is usually to keep the acidity adjusted while the solution is in use. Uptake of nutrients by the plants normally results in the composition becoming alkaline, necessitating the addition of acid.

The chief reason for the unsatisfactory growth of most plants under alkaline conditions is that many of the elements are precipitated as insoluble salts. Iron is the first to be affected, and a very alkaline solution is almost sure to be deficient in iron. Ferric ammonium citrate is a good source of iron under slightly alkaline conditions, and is often used. The effect on calcium can be off-set to some extent by increasing the amount of this element, but this in turn is likely to cause the phosphorous to form insoluble calcium phosphate, so that the last condition is worse than the first.

Except for such lime-loving plants as sweet peas, however, the golden rule is to stick to the *pH* 5–*pH* 6·5 range. Going outside this is only inviting trouble.

How do we determine the *pH*? This is quite a simple process, involving the use only of a test tube and a bottle of indicator dye.

A convenient indicator to use is that known as "678", serving, as its name indicates, for this range of *pH*. See that the tube is clean and rinse it in distilled water before use. Then dip it in the solution and rinse out at least once before going on with the test. Pour the recommended quantity of solution into the tube (10 c.c. is usual) and add the correct amount of indicator. The usual amount of indicator is 0·5 c.c., and a pipette can be provided in the stopper of the bottle to deliver this amount. Shake the test tube, holding a clean cork or piece of clean paper over the mouth, and compare the colour with the chart provided with the indicator.

pH indication books, which consist of sensitive strips of paper, one of which is torn off and used at a time, are more convenient but not so definite in reaction. The colour produced by dipping the paper in the solution is compared with colours printed on the covers of the book.

A more accurate method involves the use of a comparator. This is a small instrument with space for two tubes side by side and small holes like camera eyes in one side. On the other side is frosted glass. By looking through the holes with the light shining through the tubes from the back, the colours can be compared very accurately. The instrument has a space for a disc containing different colour standards set in a circle. As the disc is rotated, each colour comes in front of the eye in turn, and that which most nearly matches the colour of the solution indicates its *pH*. By using two different dyes (bromo-cresol purple and bromothymol blue) with the appropriate colour discs for each, the *pH* can be accurately read from *pH* 5·2 to *pH* 7·6.

Purchase of the comparator, tubes and discs, however, involves an expenditure of something like £6, against a few shillings for the single test-tube method, and may not be considered justified.

Growers on a big scale sometimes use an electrical conductivity tester which costs £30 or so, and is remarkably convenient and accurate. Such apparatus is of course only to be considered if a really big installation is concerned.

MANAGEMENT OF SOLUTIONS

There are several ways of maintaining a constant *pH*.

Addition of Alkali. This, of course, is if the solution is too acid—*pH* 5·5, or below. Potassium hydroxide is often recommended, but I have found sodium hydroxide quite convenient and effective. This is bought in pellets, which are kept in a tightly stoppered bottle, as they soon absorb moisture. The method is this:

If the quantity of solution to be adjusted is very small, dissolve one pellet in half a pint of water. Add a small measured quantity (a fluid ounce will do) to the solution, stir, and again test the *pH*. If not enough, go on adding a similar quantity of alkali solution until the correct reading is obtained. Stir well each time, as it will take a little while for the hydroxide to spread throughout the solution.

If the quantity to be dealt with is larger—say ten gallons or more—add one pellet, and take the *pH* again. If it is still too acid, add more hydroxide, pellet by pellet, again stirring each time, until the correct reading is reached.

Unfortunately there is no practicable method of calculating from the *pH* how much hydroxide to add, and then adding this amount at one time. The addition of successive amounts of liquid or pellets is tedious at first, but cannot be avoided.

After a little experience, however, a fairly accurate guess can be made, and the *pH* brought near the desired reading with one addition. The final adjustment is then made as already described.

Remember that the hydroxide is caustic. The solution must not be allowed to get on the hands or clothes. The pellets can be safely handled with dry fingers, but not if the hands are wet. Nor should they be held too long, as the moisture absorbed will cause a solution to be in contact with the skin.

Addition of acid. This is the adjustment that usually has to be made. Sulphuric acid is the best acid to add, and the cheaper, commercial grade is all that is required.

As in the case of alkalies, dilute adjusting liquid is made. For ten gallons of solution, or less, a 10 per cent. solution of acid (4 fluid ounces in two pints of water); for 10 to 50 gallons, a 20 per cent. solution is indicated (8 fluid ounces in two pints) and for larger amounts a 50 per cent. concentration (one pint of acid plus one pint of water).

Do not forget that sulphuric acid is a dangerous liquid. It must be handled with care, and the acid always added slowly to the water, not the water to the acid. If a drop of acid should by chance get spilled on the skin, wash it off quickly with plain water.

Ammonium sulphate. Inclusion of this chemical in the composition of the solution has what is called a buffering effect. Plants take up the ammonium ion more rapidly than the sulphate ion, which is left behind.

As the sulphate ion is acidic, it tends to counteract the alkalinity which develops in solutions as the nitrate ion is absorbed. The value of ammonium sulphate, however, is limited because too much of it in a solution upsets growth.

Phosphate level. Some works on soilless culture have recommended increasing the amount of phosphorous in the solution to maintain slightly acid conditions. It is true that this has the required effect, but too much phosphorous often causes a deficiency of iron.

Until experience is gained, the *pH* of the solution should be checked every day. Afterwards it can be left to twice a week, unless there is reason to think that rapid change is occurring.

Whatever container is used, large tank or small pot, the level of the water should be made up with plain water each day. Strong-growing plants in hot summer weather will use up to 30 per cent. of the volume of solution in one day. The solution that is left is naturally much more concentrated than intended, and must be restored if proper growth is to be obtained. Except in small installations, it is wise to adjust the water to be added with acid to *pH* 6 before making up the solution. If this is not done, and the water is alkaline, as is so often the case, iron and phosphorous will be precipitated out of solution. If you would like a practical instance of this, pour a few drops of alkaline water into a solution. Each drop will cause a blob of cloudiness as it enters.

The use of rain water, which tends to be neutral lessens this risk, but even in the case of rain water it is better to bring down the *pH* before additions are made.

For small units, the most practical method to use is to coat the inside of a spare tank with two coats of asphalte, and to keep in this a supply of acidified water always ready for use.

When you have gained experience and confidence, you will be able to dispense with the daily additions of water, and add it only twice a week, or even weekly. The way to do this is to use a tank much larger than the size of bed warrants. Suppose, for example, you need only a 50 gallon tank. By using a 100 gallon tank you will be able to put in much more water than you need. Let us imagine that you find in practice the solution loses five gallons a day. At the beginning of the week you add 20 more gallons, making a total of 70, which allows for four losses of five gallons. By the end of the week you will have only 35 gallons left. You have thus gone from too much to too little water, but the average has been about the right amount.

The weekly method is more labour-saving, but the safest way is to add water daily, at any rate until you are satisfied you are so skilful that you can be sure of not affecting the growth.

What you are doing in effect is to go from too dilute a solution to too concentrated a solution. As concentration causes hardening of growth it is apparent that it is easy to cause hardening if the concentration is allowed to become too high for too long.

Concentration, however, is a useful method of control if it desired deliberately to harden the plant, either for planting out from nursery beds or because growth has become too soft.

It can be done either by allowing the solution volume to decrease by withholding water additions, or by increasing the quantity of salts added when making up the solution. It is possible to double, or even treble the total amounts of salts used, provided they are kept in the same proportion. Such a practice, however, would only be likely to be of benefit in the depths of winter when plants require little water. The more concentrated the solution, the less water there is available to be taken up, and it is possible for plants to wilt from lack of moisture even though their roots are immersed in solution.

The concentration of solutions is expressed by what is called osmotic pressure, which is read in atmospheres. The useful range of osmotic pressure for good growth is 0·5 to 2·0 atmospheres, with a fair average for most conditions of about one atmosphere.

Apparatus is on the market for measuring the osmotic pressure of solutions, but is very expensive, and like the *pH* instruments, could only be justified on a very large scale. For the average grower, even on a commercial scale, the use of the right amount of chemicals in making up and maintaining a solution is all that is necessary.

Just as concentrating a solution is at times useful, so dilution can also be done deliberately for special purposes.

MANAGEMENT OF SOLUTIONS

Seedlings, for example, are usually more successful if they are fed with solution at one-half strength. Maturer plants also benefit from weaker solutions in very hot dry weather.

Before you venture on these practices, however, it should be remembered that the strength of a solution can be decreased as rapidly as you like without harm, but that it should be increased *only by degrees*.

You can, for example, empty out your solution and substitute plain water without harm, provided the plants are not left without nutrients too long. But if you suddenly double or treble the concentration, wilting is very likely to occur until the roots become accustomed to the new conditions.

Consideration of this question of changes in the composition of nutrient solutions leads us to one of the most controversial problems in the whole of soilless culture. It is obvious that after a solution is freshly made, if the same solution is used continually, important changes occur in the composition as the plants take up the various nutrients. Strong-growing tomato plants, for example, can absorb half the amount of nitrogen in an average solution in six days.

Before the end of a week, then, the solution will be a very different one. Half the nitrogen might be gone. Perhaps a quarter of the potassium and phosphorous, and so on. By the end of another week the solution is very much more out of balance, and by the end of yet another week is beyond redemption.

If any sort of control is to be kept, it is obvious that some method must be found of replacing the nutrients that are taken up. This is done by chemical analysis of the solution to find what has been taken up, and by replacing it with fresh salts. In this way, if the tests and additions are properly made, a solution can be kept in constant use for a year or more, and still provide a good growing medium.

These tests, for anyone with chemical knowledge, are fairly simple. With practice all the necessary tests can be done by devoting a few hours a week to the task.

But there are very serious drawbacks to the system. To begin with, the cost of the apparatus is heavy. With prices what they are today, even the barest minimum of apparatus costs £80 to £100. To carry out the tests properly, some kind of laboratory with running water must be available, which rules out the average household. The bathroom or garage sink can be used, but these are only makeshifts leading to inaccurate work.

Moreover, this initial expense, heavy as it is, is not all. Breakages of apparatus occur. Reagents deteriorate and must be renewed. Interest widens and further tests are undertaken, leading to more apparatus and more bills.

Furthermore, constant watchfulness is necessary to maintain a high degree of accuracy. Some of the dilutions used in testing are so great that even a tiny error in testing becomes multiplied to a big one in practice. An error of two parts per million in testing for magnesium, for example, can become 20 p.p.m. or more when the result is worked out. And as this amounts to nearly half the total of magnesium in the solution, the effect can be to throw the whole solution out of balance.

Nor are these errors easy to avoid. Reagents have a habit of insidiously deteriorating, and they have to be checked against a solution of known strength frequently, which means a good deal of work. Every time a fresh reagent is made up it has to be tested in the same way, since a supply from a different source may lead to an appreciable difference in result.

Finally, some of the most vital tests are hardly possible to the average non-chemist grower at all. Boron, for example, requires extra apparatus and especial care, as even the glass of an ordinary bottle can cause boron to make its appearance in what should be pure distilled water.

Another argument against testing is that even with skilled and complete testing, the composition of the water supply may be such as to lead to gradual build-ups in the solution of unwanted ions for which tests are not carried out. Sodium is a possibility in point. There are other and more obscure elements whose presence in an isolated quantity of water is negligible, but which, when the water is continually added, and the element is allowed to accumulate, can cause trouble.

So although I have used these tests for years, by and large my considered opinion is that for the average gardener or grower it is unwise to attempt them. Only if you are well versed in chemistry, or so deeply interested that you *must* know what goes on chemically in your solution or your growing medium, would it be worth while.

For this reason, I have not attempted to give the details of the chemical tests in this book. There are several published works on the subject, some of which appear in the bibliography at the end of this book, and full instructions on the methods are available there. But remember—you have been warned!

There is one exception to this view of the practical value of chemical tests for the everyday grower. That is the phosphorous test. This is so useful for the treatment of calcareous sand and gravel that it can be well justified if this type of aggregate is concerned. Fortunately the phosphorous test is one of the most straightforward of all, involving only a small amount of apparatus. Details of the operation are given in the chapter on sand culture.

Having burned my boats, as far as periodic testing is

concerned, then, I can hear a hundred readers protesting: "Must we, then, let the solution become unbalanced?"

Not necessarily. There are three ways out of the difficulty.

1. By adopting a system whereby the solution is used only once. The overhead watering of sand beds is such a system.

2. By changing the solution, if used continually, often enough to ensure that the composition does not alter too greatly before renewal takes place.

3. By studying the nutrient uptake of a given crop under given conditions, and using this as a basis for feeding each successive crop under the same conditions.

The first method is the one which has been adopted by most of the growers in the British Isles. It is the one sure way of avoiding trouble as far as the composition of the solution is concerned, and it is one of the chief advantages of the sand method.

Method number two is open to all growers whose installations are not so big that a complete change every fortnight or three weeks is too wasteful an undertaking. It is quite practicable for the ordinary garden greenhouse and even small commercial venture. And of course it is by far the best way with pot plants in the house. Nor is it quite such a labour as might at first appear. While in the height of summer it is wiser to discard the old solution and make up afresh every fortnight, in the spring and autumn three weeks is often enough and in the winter once a month.

The third method is only open to those who have had

the time and facilities for detailed study over a number of years. Let us take an illustration. Suppose you have been growing Ailsa Craig tomatoes by soilless culture over several seasons, analysing each week. By keeping careful records you know that with plants of a certain size in certain weather conditions they are likely to use up a certain number of parts per million of each element each week. The time comes when by going on your experience of previous seasons, you can make up a solution and then go on adding week by week the amounts of salts you know are going to be required.

If you arrange matters properly, it should be possible to grow good crops for a whole season, testing only once or twice as a check on your calculations. But it can only be done by the shrewdest of cultivators, and then only if the variety, the situation and the weather are fairly constant.

It would be a great convenience if plants always took up the same amounts of elements in a given period. Then we should only have to look up a ready-reckoner to know what to add to a solution.

There are some who maintain that a particular variety of a particular plant always takes up the elements *in the same proportion*, averaged over a given period of growth. The *amounts* may vary, but the *proportion*, they say, is always the same. If then, by one simple test, the concentration could be determined, all that would be necessary would be to add more solution, already compounded, until the correct strength is reached.

This, I believe, I am at liberty to say, is what is behind the statement in the *Carnation Year Book* for 1950, "research workers are experimenting to prepare a solution in order to avoid the usual fortnightly analysis, about which details of course cannot yet be given".

But even if the experiments are successful, a great deal of work would have to be done to establish the exact requirements of all the crops which might be required to be grown, and when one thinks of the hundreds of varieties of even one plant, the task looms up a colossal one.

No, as yet it is simpler to change completely, after all.

7

WATER CULTURE

IN the late 1920's water culture was the first of the soilless culture systems to catch the public eye, and in some ways it still offers advantages with which no other system can compete.

It is the only method in which no solid material is in contact with the roots. In the opinion of Dr. Gericke, the chief "prophet" of the system, it is the only really soilless system. He claims that the gravel, sand and other aggregates sometimes used are actually modified soil systems, except that the "soil" used is some inert material.

One of the chief advantages of water culture has only recently come to light. Gravel, sand, cinders, and the other aggregates all have the property of "adsorption"—that is, they lock up on their surfaces nutrients taken out of the solution. These nutrients are in a form which it is sometimes difficult to leach out with water or even dilute acid, yet which is partially available to the roots of the plant.

As the cinders (or whatever material is being used) adsorb more and more nutrient from the constant contact with solution, they gradually acquire enough to throw the feeding of the plant out of balance.

The process, of course, depends on many factors, including the strength of the solution and the number of leachings, as well as the type of aggregate and the type of plant. But on an average, after three years, trouble through excessive amounts of one or more elements may be experienced.

To make this clearer, suppose a solution is being fed which contains 60 p.p.m. phosphorous. Suppose also that the aggregate is an old one, and that on its surfaces nutrients containing the equivalent of 100 p.p.m. P have been adsorbed. Not all of that will be available to the plant, but enough might be taken up, let us say, to release 30 p.p.m. to the roots, and so make up the total parts per million P available up to 90 p.p.m. Such a high concentration of phosphorous would throw the whole solution out of balance, particularly with regard to iron.

Water culture offers no such disadvantages. There are no solid particles to present a surface to the solution on which nutrients can be adsorbed. For this reason some of the latest soilless culture workers have suggested a kind of happy medium between water culture and gravel culture. In principle it involves supporting the plant in a bed of gravel, with the major portion of the roots going down below to a water culture tank in which, however, the solution does not remain continuously, but is pumped to and fro as in the normal gravel unit.

In the meantime water culture continues to attract its adherents, and also its critics. And so as to suit either, what follows will be strictly factual.

Almost any type of watertight container can be used for water culture. They fall roughly into three classes:

> *Small experimental units.* Quart fruit jars are the best. They are fitted with a cork, in which two holes are bored, one with an extension reaching to the side of the cork like a keyhole. The sketch gives the idea.
>
> One hole is for the aeration tube, and the other—the "keyhole" one—for the plant stem. It is slid

WATER CULTURE 57

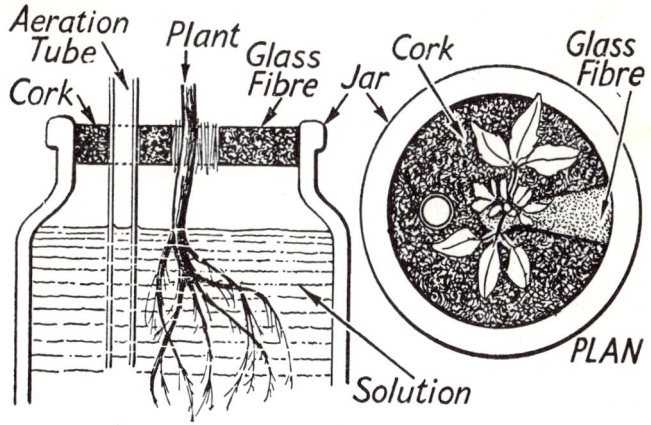

along the "keyhole" and supported with glass wool packed round so as to hold it firmly in place.

Greenhouse and garden units. Any larger type of china, wood or metal vessel is suitable for this. Old kitchen sinks or ammunition boxes are often used. They can be of any length or width, but should be six to eight inches deep. Special tanks of this depth can be made out of metal, asbestos cement, wood, plastic—or indeed almost any material. A very convenient size is four feet long by two feet wide. Any number of such units can be coupled up by means of piping.

Large-scale units. As wood is so hard to get, and metal so expensive, tanks for water culture on a commercial scale are usually made of cement or cement-faced brick. Concrete is also used. Black iron is occasionally found, but cannot be said to be a commercial proposition.

Whichever type of tank is used, it should have a double coat of asphalte or asphalte paint. The finest covering of this kind is made by heating lump petroleum asphalte (free of tar) until it runs freely, and then spraying or painting on.

For the ordinary gardener, however, this is a difficult and tedious process, since unless the tank is pre-heated the asphalte congeals as soon as it is applied. It can be spread laboriously by means of a brush and blow-lamp applied almost simultaneously, but takes a long time and involves quite a risk of burnt fingers. Fortunately, however, there are several grades of tar-free asphalte paint on the market which can be applied cold like ordinary paint, and they are perfectly satisfactory if a good coat is applied, allowed to dry, and then repeated.

Fruit jars need not be asphalted, but thick brown paper should be wrapped round and tied with string or rubber bands to keep out light from the roots. China or porcelain enamel vessels also need no other covering. But the enamel must be complete, without holes or scratches.

After the container or tank itself, the next consideration is the plant bed. In the case of the fruit jar, this consists of the perforated cork. In the case of small tanks, lids of plywood, asbestos cement, or similar substance can be made to fit on top and pierced with holes about two inches across into which corks can be fitted just as in the case of the jars.

On larger tanks the usual type of bed is a wooden frame fitted just over the edge of the tank. Nailed or wired to the frame is heavy chicken wire of about one-half to one-inch mesh, stretched tightly so as to have as small a sag as possible. If ungalvanised wire can be obtained, this is better. But usually galvanised wire is the only kind to hand, and this must be carefully painted with two coats of asphalte, so that the zinc in the galvanising, which is highly toxic, does not come into contact with the solution or the roots.

If the tank is a wide one, cross-stays may be necessary across the tank to provide extra support. The bed frame must also be constructed so that it is not too high above the tank. It should be just above the solution level when the tank is full. At least one section of the tank should be left uncovered, and a smaller, detachable bed constructed to fit the gap. This can then be lifted to inspect the solution and roots, and also to add chemicals and take samples for testing pH.

Next comes the plant bed itself, which rests on top of the wire. The usual thickness is three to four inches, but for potatoes and root crops it has to be deeper.

The principle of the bed is that it should be large enough in texture not to slip down between the mesh of the chicken wire; close enough to retain moisture and offer some support to the plant stem, soft enough not to damage the plants, and not so soggy as to lead to trouble through too wet conditions. Materials that have been used to obtain these conditions include peat moss, peat moss and excelsior (wood shavings), sawdust, rice hulls, and glass wool. If small seeds are sown in the bed, the mixture of some sand with the moss is beneficial. But in any case the material must not pack so tightly as to exclude life-giving air. For the same reason, the bottom of the bed, or portions of it, must not be allowed to sag down into the solution, otherwise waterlogging will follow.

It is easier to germinate seeds in seed-boxes of soil or sand and transplant them to the bed, but seed may be sown direct if required. Tubers and bulbs may of course be planted direct in any case.

When plants are transplanted from seed-boxes to the beds they must be arranged with the roots as low as possible so that they grow down into the solution as soon as conditions permit. To assist this, the solution level should be about half an inch from the bottom of the bed. As the roots grow larger the level my be allowed to fall to several inches below, depending on the size of the root system. In the interval between the roots being inserted in the bed and the time they reach the solution, great care must be used to keep the bed as moist as is necessary to ensure good growth without over-watering.

The "happy medium" of moisture is also the aim when seeds are sown direct in the bed. Too much will cause rotting of the seed: too little will result in patchy germination and dying off after the primary roots are formed.

The two chief difficulties of water culture are supporting the plants and aerating the solution.

Plant support. Natural soil provides both a root anchorage and actual physical support to the stem in cases where earthing up is practised. The water culture bed scarcely does either. Well-compounded bed material offers some kind of support for the smaller plants, but the larger ones are always flopping over, presenting a very ragged and uneven appearance, even if no actual harm is being done. Tall plants like tomatoes offer even more difficulty. Canes cannot be used, since unless they are wired or strung individually to the wire of the bed, they cannot be supported at the bottom.

So the stringing method is the only alternative, though even here it is far too easy to loop the end of the string too firmly round the stem, with the result that the weight of the plant itself may tend to pull it out of the bed. This constant fiddling with flopping plants has discouraged more water culture gardeners than anything else, and yet I know of no real answer to the problem. With experience, a good deal of ingenuity can be attained in overcoming this difficulty of support, but that is the most encouragement I can offer.

Aeration. Despite statements to the contrary, there is no real doubt that still solutions do not provide enough oxygen for best growth. Aeration of the solution in some way is indispensable if really good results are to be obtained. Plants whose oxygen requirements are not high can be grown satisfactorily, obtaining their oxygen through the porous bed and the roots suspended in the moist air between the bed and the solution, but even these would be improved with proper aeration.

So if you want to make sure, it is best to assume that anything you decide to grow would appreciate air, and to take some special steps to provide it.

There are three main methods of aeration.

(1). By bubbling air through the solution. With single plants in fruit jars, this is done by inserting a glass tube through the hole in the cork so that the bottom rests nearly at the bottom of the jar. Air can then be blown down it either by mouth (a finicky business); by a cycle pump or something similiar (but be careful not to push the plant pot over when working the pump) or by a small aquarium aeration pump (which is very neat and satisfactory).

The aeration pump can be coupled up by means of rubber tubing to any numbers of jars, and provides a steady stream of small bubbles that are ideal for the job.

In larger systems larger aeration pumps can be used, but the bubbling must not be so violent as to disturb the roots and cause damage.

(2). By circulation of the solution. This also has the advantage of ensuring thorough dissolving and mixing of chemicals put into the solution. If heat is applied at one central point, warmed solution can be circulated through any number of connected tanks, which is very beneficial under some conditions. The expense of keeping a pump going continuously, however, has to be carefully considered.

(3). By a cascade. If a pump is provided which sends the solution up in the form of a fountain, falling back again into the tank, it forms a cascade, which brings the water into contact with a large amount of air, some of which is dissolved. The same effect can be produced by circulating the solution over a miniature waterfall.

The two latter systems of aeration are of course only practicable in large installations.

Management of the solution in water culture depends more on the type of plant being grown than it does with any other system of soilless growth. After the root system has been led down to the solution as already explained, the level is allowed to fall to not more than three inches below the bottom of the bed.

The larger the space between the upper surface of the solution and the bottom of the bed the better the aeration, within limits. After that the roots tend to dry off and die.

In large installations it may be economical to test the solution at intervals and add chemicals as required. In most cases, it is better to change the solution completely at intervals. The time between these intervals depends chiefly on the season of growth and upon the mineral content of the water being used. If it is high summer and plants are growing apace, they will be using up nutrients

POTATOES

Seed-sowing. The potato requires a deeper seed-bed than almost any other popular crop. First, place a layer of coarse material direct on the wire netting, about an inch thick. On top rest the tubers, or parts of tubers if they have been cut. On top of the tubers add another four inches of bedding material, which in this case may be of a more open texture than with most crops.

Growing on. Give the bed a good soaking after planting and it should remain sufficiently moist to last until the tops begin to show through. Afterwards the only special point to watch is that the tubers do not grow out of the bed, in which case they become green and poisonous. Add more material on top if any sign of this is seen.

TURNIPS

Seed-sowing. A seed-bed two inches deep is quite enough. Sow the seed directly in this, just covered with a thin layer of material.

Growing on. Iron deficiency is particularly possible because of the rapid growth of the plant. If it is noticed, and cannot be rectified by additions to the solution, spraying a very weak solution of ferrous sulphate direct on to the leaves may be tried. It should be washed off again in a short time with plain water.

Radishes and beetroot are grown in the same way.

more quickly, and will require a more frequent change of solution. Once a week or ten days would be quite in order. If it is winter or autumn, less frequent changing is called for—say, once a fortnight, to once every three weeks.

The water supply affects the question in this way. If the supply is comparatively pure, little else other than what you put into the solution will be there. If, on the other hand, the water has a high natural salt content, build-ups of the naturally occurring elements will be going on, and the solution will become unbalanced more quickly than if the purer water were being used. This is one of the reasons for preferring rain water to other supplies. If rapid build-ups are known to be likely, it is better to be on the safe side and change the solution weekly.

One method of cutting down the number of changes is to use a much deeper tank than is necessary for growth. If, for example the tank is twelve inches deep instead of six, there will be twice the volume of solution for the roots to call upon, and its composition will change correspondingly more slowly.

Twice the amount of chemicals, however, will have to be added in the first place, and if any automatic aeration or pumping is done, twice the electrical effort will have to be put in to achieve the same result. So the final result is only to cut down the process of weighing and dissolving the chemicals.

Solution mixing in water culture requires a special technique to ensure good results. The tank should first be filled about half full, and then each different salt added at a different part of the tank. The remainder of the water is then put in, preferably with a hose directed in one direction so that the solution circulates round as it fills up.

"Topping up" is done in the same way, but do not forget that if the water to be added is alkaline, it should be acidified to the correct pH before adding.

Ensuring sufficient iron for the plants is apt to be a common problem. Usually iron solution has to be added twice a week. This can be sprayed on the bed, falling through into the solution, at the same time leaving some available for absorption by the roots in the bed, or by adding direct to the solution. Symptoms of iron deficiency are given in a later chapter. They should be watched for closely until sufficient experience has been obtained to feel confident that the plants are not suffering in this respect. On the other hand, do not be so lavish with the iron that a phosphorous deficiency is induced.

Reference has already been made to the possibility of warming solutions to improve growth. The usual temperature recommended is five degrees above the temperature of the air in which the crop is being grown.

Even if the solution is not warmed, special care should be taken to see that in cooler weather the water being used to make up the solution or to top it up, is not too cold. The chill at least should be taken off, either by the addition of a bucket or two of hot water, or by the use of water which has stood in the sun or in the home or greenhouse. This is more important in water culture than with other systems, because the solution is in immediate and constant contact with the roots, whereas in sand or gravel the contact is intermittent.

There is a special technique for many crops in water culture. The recommendations which follow are not necessarily the only way to obtain good results, but at least they are the result of experience which has passed the acid test: "Does it work?"

TOMATOES

Seed-sowing. In sand or soil in the ordinary way.

Planting. Take up the plants with a small soil ball attached; make a hole in the seed bed so that the bottom of the soil rests just above the bottom of the bed, and firm the bed material round the soil so as to give as much support as possible.

Growing on. The roots should be down into the solution within a fortnight. If their rate of growth makes this seem unlikely, add dilute solution to the bed itself (half-strength) until the plant begins to look "happy". Do not overdo this bed nourishment, otherwise the roots will not bother to go down into the solution (sheer laziness!). When the roots are established, gradually allow the solution level to fall to about two inches below the bottom of the bed.

CUCUMBERS

Because of their high water requirement, cucumbers often do better in water culture than in any other way.

Seed-sowing. As in soil.

Planting. In the same way as tomatoes, except that greater care must be taken to see that the young plant never goes short of water. Warmed solution is of special benefit.

Growing on. Spraying of the plants with warm water is of the greatest value. Be sure, however, that cold water is not used. With the humid conditions already present, cold moisture is inviting mildew.

CARROTS

Seed-sowing. Sow directly in the bed. Trans-planting carrots is almost impossible.

Growing on. A bed three inches deep is necessary. If long varieties are to be grown, they will go down well below the seed-bed, and the mesh of the wire will have to be larger to permit them to develop without distortion. The addition of sand to the bed to provide closer and moister conditions is a good thing. Later on, however, the bed should be kept on the dry side to discourage too many side roots.

ONIONS

Seed-sowing. Equally good results are obtained from sowing the seed direct in the bed, or by using seedling plants. The chief precaution is not to let the slender plants slip through into the solution below.

Growing on. The danger in soil of developing "thick neck" because the bulblets buried too deeply is not often encountered in water culture. For this reason it is actually easier to grow good onions than in soil.

The bulb itself acts as a plant support, so that this problem is also solved. Altogether a most satisfactory crop for water culture!

CABBAGE

Seed-sowing. Best done in soil.

Planting. Take out a hole in the seed-bed, and plant the seedling with a small ball of soil. Do not cut off the tap root as when transplanting into soil. In the normal way there will be enough roots already developed in the seed-box or nursery bed to be able to place some into the solution straight away.

Growing on. Root development with cabbage is usually very rapid. The chief point to watch is that the level of solution is allowed to fall as soon as possible, since the better the aeration, the greater the effect on growth.

Cauliflower, kale and similar plants are grown in the same way.

LETTUCE

Seed-sowing. Make a bed two inches deep, and sow the seeds half an inch deep in this. Sow thickly, as in soil, and thin when the plants show through.

Growing on. Chief difficulty is in getting the small roots to "jump" the half-inch space between the bottom of the bed and top of the solution. This should be achieved by the time the plants are two inches or so high.

Encouragement of downward root growth is achieved by:

1. Keeping the bed on the dry side.

2. Applying no nutrients to the bed.

3. Warming the solution if necessary.

The chief danger is mildew from having too wet a seed-bed. Once botritis has started it can spread very rapidly through the crop under water culture conditions.

PEAS AND BEANS

These are among the easiest and most satisfactory crops to grow by water culture.

Seed-sowing. The bed should be two to four inches deep, and can be as coarse as you like. In fact, the easy-going tolerance of these seeds to whatever type of bed they are subjected is one of the reasons for their popularity. I have even seen lawn mowings used very suitably! Sow direct in the bed in rows as in soil.

Growing on. The plants can be set a little closer than in soil. Principal problem is the old one of support. The simplest method is to set four posts at each corner of the bed and wire them across, as do the carnation growers. Strings can then be tied from the wires down on to the mesh of the wire at the bottom of the bed. String nets are also good.

The seed-bed, being coarse, will stand a good deal of moisture. There is no danger of lack of aeration, since the solution level can be kept as low as four inches below the bed when the plants are in full growth, providing a larger air space.

STRAWBERRIES

Planting. Use a large-mesh wire for the bed, and plant the crowns with the roots in the solution immediately Very little depth of bed is necessary.

Growing on. Keep the bed almost perfectly dry, on the surface, otherwise crown rot is a danger. Only sufficient moisture to keep alive the lateral roots in the bed should be given.

ANNUAL FLOWERS

All these are grown the same way, except that the size of the root system determines the depth of the bed. Pansies, for example, have the smallest root system, and need only a shallow bed. Snap-dragons, carnations, marigolds, and similar sized plants need about three to four inches. Delphiniums, sweet-peas, and hollyhocks must be grown in beds four to six inches deep.

Seed-sowing. Sow in boxes in soil and transplant when several inches high.

Planting. Plant direct on the wire netting with soil root system still attached, and then add most of the bed material *on top* and around the stems. This will encourage vigorous side-rooting and in consequence better aeration and support.

Growing on. The solution at first should be within half an inch of the bottom of the bed. Then let it fall until the proper height is reached. This again will depend on the size of the roots

BULBS AND CORMS

If I were asked to suggest to someone absolutely new to soilless culture a good crop to start on, I think I should suggest bulbs in water culture.

So much food is already stored in the bulbs that almost anyone can obtain good results even if their solution is not right. In fact, this used to be much better known than it is today. Not so long ago bulb glasses, in which bulbs grew in water alone, were a common sight in drawing-rooms. What a pity water culture was not known then!

Planting. Seed-beds should be about four inches deep, and the bulb should "sit" about half an inch above the bottom of the bed. See that the bulb stays upright when pressing down the bed material round it.

Growing on. Daffodils produce the longest roots—about six inches long. Hyacinths are about four inches, and tulips up to three. In keeping with the statement above, the bulbs do not seem to bother whether the solution is applied above, on the seed-bed, or in the solution.

Corms, rhizomes (iris), and tubers (dahlia) may all be grown the same way. A useful method of support for the taller of these flowers, such as gladioli and dahlias, is to spread a piece of four-inch wire mesh over the bed and raise it as the plants grow taller. For the beginner, the iris is perhaps the best plant to recommend, as like the bulbs, it is not very particular.

BEGONIAS

Begonias are such lovely flowers, and so fine when properly grown, that I am including a special section all to themselves, although they ought really to be grouped with the tubers.

Planting. Use beds about four inches deep topped with a thin layer of soil. Keep the bed very moist at first. In fact, this is the one exception of which I have personal knowledge—you can allow the solution to touch the seed-bed if you like. When the bed is thoroughly wet, lower the solution again.

Growing on. Apply solution both directly to the bed as well as below. Begonias have a very small root system, and their upper roots play an important part in their nourishment. Iron need not be applied as frequently as with other plants. As in soil, they should be kept in a fairly shady place.

SUCCULENTS

Although succulents are popularly supposed to grow without water to all intents and purposes, they have actually been successfully grown in water culture. M. Deschamps, a French experimenter, has been successful with phyllocactus epiphyllim, opuntia, and echinopsis, among others. He used the fruit jar method and his solution for major elements was:*

Rain water	10 litres
Mono-potassium phosphate	2 gr. 70
Calcium nitrate	9 gr. 10
Magnesium sulphate	4 gr. 40
Ammonium sulphate	0 gr. 82

Trace elements were as usual.

*From the French periodical "*Cactus.*"

[Graphic Photo Union

Lettuces by sub-irrigation. The beaker operates
a trip-switch for stopping pumping automatically.

Glass wool on
gravel beds
i n c r e a s e s
light for car-
nations.

[Graphic Photo Union

The author tending one of his crops of tomatoes. These were grown in a brick bed containing cinders.

3 [Birmingham Evening Despatch

4

A prize-winning truss from the crop shown above.

5 [Graphic Photo Union

Experimental bed covering for carnations — this time asbestos.

Young cucumbers growing in a gravel bed. Frequent pumping is vital for this moisture-loving crop.

[A. N. Products

Apparatus need not be elaborate. This solution container is an old oil drum. It is raised and lowered to irrigate the small gravel bed. The grower is a Staffordshire schoolmaster who also runs a soilless culture group at his school.

Soilless culture beds in a Yorkshire greenhouse. The beds consist of separate tanks in series. The filling is sand and peat.

[W. H. Carr-Birkbeck

The end of a good crop in gravel. This material is easily cleaned and sterilised.

A truss of Stonor's Exhibition tomatoes that won first prize at a Midland show.

Soilless culture needs more apparatus than soil. Here are metal growing beds, feed tank, pipes and valves.

Young tomato plants in pots of sand. They are fed by overhead watering

[W. H. Carr-Birkbeck

[Imperial Chemical Industries

13   [*Imperial Chemical Industries*

A fish aquarium was converted to grow these tomatoes by water culture.

The drip feed. Solution percolates through the glass tube (bottom of picture).

14

Root development is excellent in sand.

15   [*F. S. Cubitt*

A typical hobby outfit for sub-irrigation. The tank at the side is raised and lowered for feeding.

|A. N. Products

|A. N. Products

A larger growing tray with feed channel and drainage spout. Such trays are excellent for raising plants.

A window-box soilless culture unit containing both seedlings and older plants

|A. N. Products

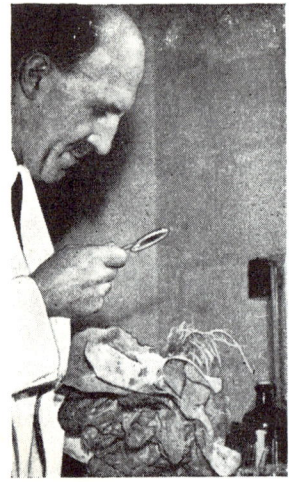

19   [Graphic Photo Union

Mr. S. R. Mullard, the soilless culture pioneer, examines a lettuce root.

An armful of first quality sand-grown carnations.

20   [Blackpool Evening Gazette

21   [F. S. Cubitt

Soilless culture is valuable in hot climates. These are cauliflowers seven weeks after planting out in Calcutta.

8

SAND CULTURE

SAND culture is the cheapest system of soilless culture to instal and the simplest to run. That is why it is the most popular method, certainly in the British Isles, and probably abroad. Most of the commercial soilless growers use sand beds, and I should imagine a majority of amateur growers as well.

Sand culture needs neither water-tight beds nor pumps, as do water culture and gravel culture. Tanks do not have to be levelled, nor piping and valves fixed. If need be, all that is really necessary is a rough rectangle of boards placed direct on the ground.

In operation, the sand system is much more tolerant of mistakes than are other methods. Up to a point, excesses and deficiencies that would cause serious trouble in water or gravel appear to be modified so that their worst effects are avoided. To the ordinary gardener, too, sand looks and feels much like ordinary soil. It is much more familiar and "natural", and he therefore takes to it more easily. Finally, sand is usually much more easily obtained than some of the media used in gravel culture methods.

But it is this very ease of obtaining the materials which has led to some of the biggest disappointments in sand culture.

For the fact is, that sand is not such a simple material as it seems.

There is silica sand and calcareous (chalky) sand. There is red sand, yellow sand, silver sand. There is sand so coarse it is really fine gravel, and there is sand so fine it is like table salt. There is sand which contains a large amount of clayey and organic matter, and there is sand which contains none at all.

Unfortunately, many of these sands are unsuitable for sand culture. The ideal sand is silica sand, so coarse that water drains freely through it, but not so coarse that it does not retain moisture. The ideal sand should contain no clay or other non-sandy matter. It should be easily available in your locality, and cheap to obtain.

It is fairly safe to predict that you will almost never find something that fulfils all those conditions. Either it is everything you want, but so far away as to make the cost of transporting it prohibitive, or everything you don't want, and so near as to be almost on your doorstep. Nevertheless, you must try and find the nearest compromise, and make do with that.

Fortunately, there are ways of turning unsuitable sand into a condition in which it can be used. If it is too fine, mix small pebbles with it ("half-inch round" is the trade term) until it passes what I call the "flower pot" test. Almost fill a flower pot with the sand, and pour water on in a stream from a watering can without a rose. If the water soon drains away without puddling on the top, it is all right.

If the sand is too coarse, fine sand should be mixed with it until it reached the same condition. Small amounts can be mixed like cement, but on a commercial scale it is easier to place the materials heaped on one another in a long mound and furrow along with a motor cultivator.

Even if the physical nature of the sand is satisfactory,

it may be too chalky. The result will be too alkaline a condition, causing phosphorous deficiency and possibly iron starvation as well. The remedy for this type of sand is a thorough soaking with a strong solution of phosphate. The method of doing this is as follows:

First take a small jam-jar full of sand, and place it in a large clean jam-jar. Cover with distilled water so that the volume of water above the sand is about equal in depth to the volume of sand below. Then leave overnight. The next day take the *pH* of the water in the way described in a previous chapter. With calcareous sand you will find it somewhere in the region of *pH* 8.

Then work out the amount of monocalcium phosphate needed to make up a solution of 200 p.p.m. of phosphorous, and mix a convenient amount of this solution. Make enough to give the bed a thorough soaking. Water the solution on the bed and leave for several hours. Then test the water draining away from the sand for *pH*. If it is below *pH* 7, no further treatment is required.

If not, the process must be repeated until the *pH* of the liquid draining away is *pH* 7 or below. With very calcareous sand this may mean three or four leachings. Complete the test by checking with the jam-jar method as described above.

In the chapter on the management of solutions, I mentioned that the phosphorous test was the only one of the chemical tests likely to be of use to the ordinary gardener. The treatment of calcareous sand is one case in which it can be very useful. In addition to taking the *pH* of the drainings from the sand, you can test for the amount of phosphorous, and determine how much has been taken out of the solution and locked up in the sand. If the level of phosphorous has fallen from 200 p.p.m. to below 100, this is further confirmation that another soaking in phosphate solution is required. The way to do this phosphorous test is as follows:

PHOSPHOROUS TEST

Apparatus required:

Two one-inch diameter specimen tubes.
5 ml. bulb pipette.
2 ml. bulb pipette.
1 ml. bulb pipette.
Methylated spirit heating lamp or bunsen burner.
Comparator and Tintometer coloured disc KV.
Stop-watch or clock.
Immersion thermometer up to 50 degrees Centigrade.

Reagents required:

REAGENT No. 1. To 200 ml. distilled water add 65 ml of concentrated sulphuric acid (analytical reagent grade). Dilute to 500 ml.

REAGENT No. 2. Dissolve without heating 4·4 grams ammonium molybdate AR in 50 ml. distilled water.

Add 2·65 ml. concentrated sulphuric acid to 50 ml. of distilled water.

Mix the two solutions and make up to 125 ml. with distilled water.

Mix this 125 ml. with an equal volume of reagent No. 1 and store in an amber glass bottle.

REAGENT No. 3. Dissolve completely 1 gram of pure hydroquinone in 100 ml distilled water and add 0·06 ml. of concentrated sulphuric acid.

Keep in an amber bottle, and discard after a month.

REAGENT No. 4. Dissolve in 250 ml. of distilled water 50 grams of anhydrous sodium carbonate and 12 grams of sodium sulphite.

This reagent must be kept in a warm place to prevent it crystallising out.

METHOD. Dilute the solution to bring the estimated amount of phosphorous to 0–25 p.p.m. which equals 0–75 p.p.m. of PO_4.

Add 5 ml. of diluted solution to one of the specimen tubes.

Add to it 2 ml. of Reagent No. 2 and 1 ml. of Reagent No. 3.

Raise the temperature over the flame to between 23 and 27 degrees Centigrade.

Stand for five minutes by the stop-clock.

Add to the second specimen tube 2 ml. of Reagent No. 4.

Mix the contents of the two tubes by pouring back and forth. Bubbles will form, which can be removed by tapping sharply against the sides of the tube.

Transfer the blue solution to the right-hand tube of the comparator. Fill the other tube with the solution under test (as diluted).

Read the disc, and divide by three to convert PO_4 to P. Correct for any dilution found necessary in the first place.

It will be noted that in addition to the apparatus required for the test, certain other standard laboratory equipment is necessary, such as bottles for reagents and measuring cylinders or flasks for 50, 100 and 500 ml.

For the weighing out of reagents, a chemical balance is

also necessary. These items make the total cost of apparatus for this one test alone up to something like £30, depending on the quality of the balance bought. Many of the items, of course, would also be used in other tests. But if you are determined to be able to gauge the phosphorous content of solutions, this expenditure is unavoidable.

It is useful to be able to test not only the solution, but also the sand, for the amount of phosphorous. This is done by what is called "extracting" a solution from the sand or gravel, and then testing this extract as if it were ordinary solution. The value of this is that it enables you to tell whether the amount of phosphorous in calcareous media is dropping (which indicates that more phosphorous is needed in the solution), or rising (which indicates that less phosphorous can be used).

Extractions are done with the aid of Morgan's Extracting Solution, which is prepared as follows:

Dissolve 30 ml. of glacial acetic acid AR and 100 grams of AR sodium acetate ($CH_3CO_2Na3H_2O$) in distilled water and dilute to one litre.

Extracts are done in this way:

SAND. Place 5 grams of sand (which should be air dry) in each of six half-inch test tubes, and add to each 10 ml. of Morgan's extractant. Shake each tube vigorously for one minute exactly. Filter into a beaker. Test the filtered solution just as for an ordinary solution, except that the results must be doubled to allow for the extraction ratio, which is two to one.

CINDERS. Grind representative samples (obtained from different parts and different levels of the bed) with a pestil and mortar, down to less than 2 millimetre size. Extract this ground material just as for sand. Filter and test as before.

GRAVEL. Place a representative sample of the gravel of 100 grams weight in a 200 ml. glass beaker and pour over it 50 ml. of Morgan's extractant. Stir slowly with a glass rod for three minutes. Stand for fifteen minutes. Filter and apply the test as above. In this case the result must be halved to allow for the extraction ratio.

Although to anyone unfamiliar with chemistry, these tests must appear complicated at first reading, they are really quite within the ability of anyone with a very elementary knowledge of laboratory work. The first one or two tests will doubtless take a long time, but speed comes with practice.

As a further encouragement, it should be added that although the preparation of the reagents is perhaps a little tiresome, once these are made the test itself is the most accurate of all, and the one in which the human error is likely to be the smallest, even in the hands of an unskilled operator.

A competent chemist can practically guarantee to get the amount of phosphorous accurate to within about three per cent., which, with a solution of 100 p.p.m. is only 3 p.p.m. Such small limits enable the phosphorous situation to be watched very closely.

Some of the other chemical tests, even in a properly equipped laboratory and with practised chemists, are not to be relied upon to anything like that extent. This again is one of the reasons why the phosphorous test is the only one recommended for normal practice.

In fairness to all those who have installed and maintained successful sand culture units without chemical testing at all, it must also be added that with proper precautions and common-sense operating, testing even for phosphorous alone is not really necessary.

THE NEXT STEP

We can now assume, I think, that you have the right sand (or as near as possible) and that you are satisfied either that it is non-calcareous—or, if it is, that you have put the matter right with phosphate treatment. In this case, well begun is more than half done.

The next step is the construction of the bed itself. This is a matter with an almost infinite number of variations, but they fall into perhaps four main classes.

1. Home units in pots, vases and jars.
2. Out-of-door units.
3. Beds watered overhead.
4. Beds watered from below by sub-irrigation.

The latter two are usual in the amateur and commercial greenhouse.

HOME UNITS

Almost anything can be used for this purpose. Flower pots, bulb bowls, tins, earthenware pipes, boxes of metal or wood, meat dishes, baking pans—the list seems endless. The basic requirement is that there must be free drainage, and that if the material is corrodible it must be coated with asphalte paint. Usually a hole or holes are made in the bottom for the drainage.

As an example of this method, there is space for one type of container alone to be described in detail. Suppose we make it a flower pot. You may coat the inside with asphalte paint or not, as you please. It will not dry out so quickly if you do, which is perhaps better.

Over the bottom drainage hole, place a small piece of copper gauze, or a ball of glass wool, to stop the sand seeping out.

Fill with sand to about an inch from the brim, and test for drainage. Stand the pot on three equal-sized pebbles in a dish to collect the seepings, and your unit is complete. The simplest way to feed it is to pour the solution directly on the sand from a small jug or tin.

The biggest problem is to restrain your generosity and avoid over-feeding the plant. Push a finger in the sand and rub some particles between finger and thumb. If they feel moist, do not add solution. If dry, pour on a good dose until it begins to run out at the bottom. The amount to feed depends on so many factors that it is impossible to give any hard and fast rule as to the number and quantity of nutrient additions. You must just judge for yourself.

If you want to feed automatically, a very good system is by syphon tube. This is constructed by obtaining a length of 5 millimetre bore capillary tubing, a quart fruit jar, and a flat dish with a straight edge. The so-called chemists' Petri dishes are ideal for the purpose. With a grindstone or whetting stone, grind out a small groove in the edge of the jar to enable the tube to be slipped underneath. Invert the jar in the dish, and then with a gas flame, bend the tube first so that it goes under the edge of the jar about two inches, and then over the edge of the dish and down. The angle of the tube downwards determines the rate of flow. A steep angle will increase the flow, and a shallow one decrease it. The sketch on the next page should make this clear.

To start the apparatus, fill the jar with solution, place the dish over the top, and with a quick twist, invert the jar so that it is standing in the dish, still full. Slip the end of the tube quickly underneath. At first you will probably spill some of the solution, but after doing it a few times you will become adept. Then suck the tube till the solution comes through. It will drip slowly and regularly, using up the whole jarful in about twenty-four hours.

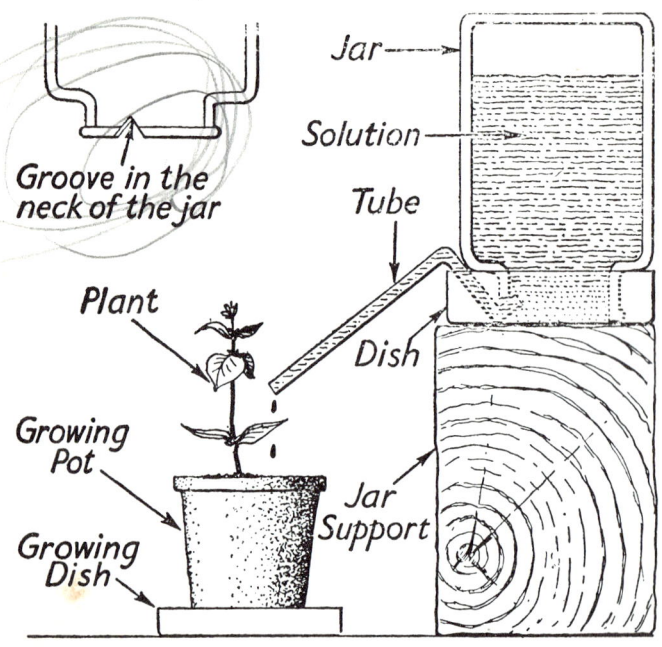

Every now and again a large bubble of air rises from below to replace the solution. It is fascinating to watch—and as it ensures good aeration of the solution, very satisfactory in practice.

See that no particles of undissolved chemicals are in the jar, or they may block the tube. If it does become blocked, soak it for a few hours in dilute sulphuric acid and then rinse through with water before replacing.

Another ingenious method for the home is the wick device. This consists of a glass wool wick up which the solution travels by capillary action. In America special wicks are made for the purpose, but I have never been able to find anyone in this country who makes them.

They can, however, be made at home by plaiting three strings of twisted glass wool strands together in a length from four to six inches long. A pot or vase with a hole in the bottom is used as a sand container. Spread out the top of the wick fan-wise so that the ends reach up into the sand and also outwards towards the sides. Fill up with sand, pouring the sand in gently so that the top of the wick is held in position and not pressed down on to the bottom of the pot. The bottom of the wick should go downwards through the hole and reach to the bottom of whatever solution container is being used. The container may be any dish with a rim of a size that will support the sand pot. I have had several designs of this sort hand-thrown on a potter's wheel, when the top and bottom can be made to fit neatly in a pleasing design. As they are hand-made, however, they are fairly expensive. If you can get them made for less than ten shillings each you will be lucky.

These wick pots are simplicity itself. All you have to do is to keep the container filled to within an inch or two of the bottom of the upper pot, and the wick will do the rest. Every fortnight change the solution and at the same time flush the sand through with tepid plain water. Be sure to use sand of the right texture. You can test this by fitting up the pot without a plant for a few days. Apply the finger and thumb test, and if the sand is nicely moist, all is well.

This type of pot has a great appeal to the housewife. It is attractive, simple, and clean, as there is no soil to fall on to the window-ledge or table and no watering required. If the bottom container is big enough, such plants can also be left for a week or two quite happily while the owner goes on holiday. Bulbs, primulas, tradescanthus, and coleus are examples of home plants that can be successfully grown in them.

OUTDOOR UNITS

These are the easiest units of all to construct. The bare requirements are an eight-inch deep bed of sand and something to keep the sand in. Usually a rough rectangle of boards held in place with pegs is enough. A stronger and more permanent structure can be made out of a double line of bricks, one on top of the other. Asbestos cement sheets cut up into eight-inch wide strips are also suitable.

If the ground below is light, no further drainage is needed. If it is heavy and clayey, a drainage pipe or two should be laid to take off excess solution.

Sections of large drainage pipes, segments of barrels, old oil drums thoroughly cleaned and asphalted and any other articles common about the average garden are all usable. Barrels and drums should be sawn or cut in two cross-wise, and bored at the bottom for drainage. If they are more than a foot deep, large stones should be placed in the bottom, and the top nine inches filled with sand. In all these types of container wads of glass wool are the best form of plugging to allow drainage and yet not let the sand seep through.

Again there is great scope for ingenuity in the application of the nutrient. The obvious method is to fill an ordinary watering can with solution and water on. Bigger beds can be fed with a hose, pouring the solution between the rows. If the solution tank is raised on wooden supports, gravity can be used to get a good flow. If on the ground or below it, a small electric or even semi-rotary hand-operated pump can be used. Drip feeds can be arranged through punctured metal or rubber pipes.

Problems peculiar to outdoor soilless culture are

chiefly concerned with drainage. Be sure that the bed is not in a natural catchment, or water from the rest of the garden will flow into it and it will always be too wet. A bed on a slight rise is best. Also pay proper regard to rain when deciding whether or not to supply nutrient. If the bed is already wet with rain, it is better to defer pouring on solution. In drip culture units these will, of course, be allowed to go on operating all the time.

Peas or sweet-peas are very successful crops to try in outdoor sand culture. For city gardens where the soil is very poor or exhausted and poisoned, these outdoor sand beds can be a great advantage and pleasure. They solve all the problems of manure, compost and humus.

BEDS FED FROM OVERHEAD

This is a popular method in commercial sand culture houses. Three principal systems are in use:

1. By hand through a hose.

2. Automatically through pipes.

3. By broadcasting nutrients dry on the surface and watering in.

The hand operated hose requires a reasonable amount of skill on the part of the operator, but is the simplest and cheapest to operate. Usually a petrol or electric pump is used to boost the solution pressure and to speed up the operation. The object is to feed evenly without undue spraying on the plants. As soon as solution is seen to be flowing out of the drainage channels, the operator moves on to the next section.

The piping system saves a good deal of labour. Again a pump is usually necessary, though with high tanks gravity may provide enough pressure. Copper, black iron, or even galvanised pipes have been successfully used. They are laid singly down the centre of narrow beds or double down each side of wider beds. Holes are pierced in the pipes at intervals, so placed that the solution comes out in a shower sufficient to cover most of the sand surface. Again feeding is done so that when the solution begins to percolate out after going through the sand, the application of solution stops.

The chief drawbacks are that unless very careful calculation is done in making the holes in the pipe, so that they gradually increase in number away from the pump, the feed is uneven. The bed portions near the pump receive more than the rest, since the solution pressure is less as the pipe lengthens.

In addition, great care has to be taken to see that the solution is finely filtered before entry into the pipe, otherwise some of the holes may become blocked and feeding become patchy. The growth of algae, the green scum sometimes seen on soil, may also cause blockage. The use of copper pipe usually prevents this, since copper inhibits algae—but copper pipe is expensive. The size usually used is half-inch or three-quarter diameter.

Some growers feed beds such as this through what is called a "Solu-feeder", which is a device for automatic mixing and dilution of nutrient solution. It does away with the space occupied by large storage tanks, since it mixes a concentrated solution with water to the required dilution while the pumping is actually in progress.

DRY NUTRIENT SYSTEM

The dry nutrient system is perhaps the simplest, and has been developed very successfully for carnations. The chemicals are weighed out, scattered evenly on top of the bed and thoroughly watered in. Only water is applied between the intervals of application of salts.

The beds for this type of culture can be made of brick, cement-faced brick, concrete, asbestos sheets, or metal or wood. The best description of the method is given by Mr. F. Hicks, of Hordle, Hampshire, in the booklet *Soilless Culture of Carnations* published by the British Carnation Society, an extract from which I quote:

"I grow in concrete beds, the sides of which are six inches high and the floor is also concrete. The floor slopes slightly towards the centre and in the centre I made a channel three inches wide. This is also concreted and in the channel lay 2-inch drain-pipes.

"The whole of the bed has a fall to one end of the house, thus giving complete drainage. It is necessary to carry the last drain-pipe through the end of the bed, and here I dug a sump to take away the drainings. Of course anyone trying this method will naturally make their own arrangements, but good drainage is very essential. There is no need to water-proof these beds, and the cost of making such a bed, including the drain-pipes, works out at 2s. 6d. per square yard. Having made the bed, fill it with a sharp washed sand to about one inch from the top. Level the sand and make sure that it is well watered; there is no need to firm it, but be certain that it is thoroughly wet. Sprinkle on the surface half-ounce per square yard of the mixture you decide to use, on the top of that (and here is an improvement over my first and second experiments) a half-inch of quarter-inch shingle—this prevents evaporation, and up to the present has completely prevented the growth of algae, which give the beds a very nice appearance. The bed will be ready for planting after two or three days. Should you have to leave it longer keep it just damp, but do not flood, for you will wash away the food you have given it. Take your plants from the propagating pit or pans and plant them straight into the beds, spacing them the same as in the ordinary way. From now on follow the ordinary method of culture apart from the feeding, the food given when the bed was made will be sufficient for the next three weeks. Of course, they will require damping down and once lightly watering in, but after three weeks begin to feed and this feeding has to be done at intervals of three weeks say for two feeds, after that every two weeks, the first and second feed a quarter of an ounce per square yard will be sufficient and thereafter a half-ounce every two weeks will keep the plants supplied with all the food they require.

"You may increase the amount during the summer months and reduce it during the winter. Here you will use your own judgment. One change you should make, and that is to increase the nitrogen content during the summer months and reduce the potash, and increase the potash during the winter months and reduce the nitrogen. The method I use of applying these salts is by sprinkling them on the surface, but owing to the very small amount used one has to mix them with a spreader in order to obtain even distribution, and up to the present I have found nothing better than dry sand. Therefore work out the area to be covered, weigh out the amount of chemicals required and thoroughly mix with dry sand, throw carefully between the rows as you would when feeding a soil bed, lightly water in. Never feed when the sand is dry and never flood immediately after feeding. There are several proved formulæ which have given good results and here is one similar to what I have used successfully: (Sufficient to make approximately 25 lb. of fertiliser)—Ammonia Sulphate, 9 lb. 12 oz; Magnesia Sulphate, 5 lb. 11 oz.; Potassium Sulphate, 1 lb. 15 oz.; Superphosphate (16 per cent.) 7 lb. 8 oz. These ingredients should be throughly mixed and finely ground. Add 1 oz. of Boric Acid and half-ounce of Ferrous Sulphate. I have never found it necessary to add any other trace elements."

SUB-IRRIGATED SAND BEDS

The technique of applying nutrients to sand beds from below by sub-irrigation we owe to Mr. J. W. Godber, of Perranporth, Cornwall, a description of whose installation is given in the chapter on commercial installations.

Briefly it consists of water-tight beds with a narrow channel at the side or in the centre consisting of asbestos cement walls an inch or so apart filled with very coarse sand or fine gravel. The solution flows along pipes and down through the channels to the bottom of the bed. From here it flows slowly to the drainage point, at the same time being drawn up through the sand by capillary action.

One of the vital factors is to have the right type of sand. It must not be too fine or too coarse, if the best results are to be obtained.

Whatever system is used, if the beds are made water-tight, the solution may be collected and re-used, although the chemicals are so cheap this is seldom done. If the beds are of the type that drain immediately either into the paths or channels, no collection arrangements are made.

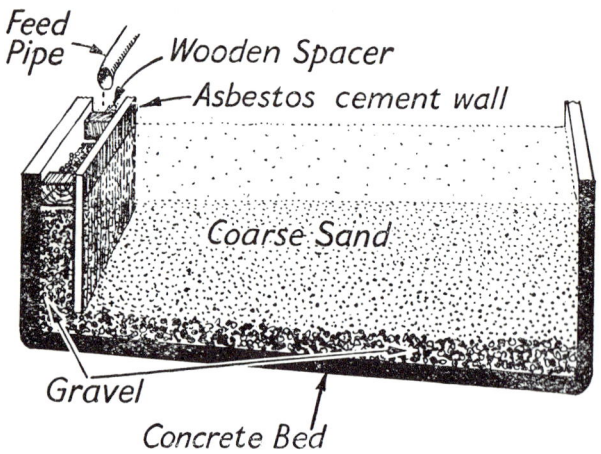

In the greenhouse either raised beds or ground beds may be constructed. The latter are much less trouble and expense. But any normal greenhouse bench is suitable. In this case the free drainage type of bed is preferable, as it is more difficult to convert a soil bench to the watertight condition necessary. In any case the minimum depth of sand should be six inches, and up to eight inches is better. Coarse sand or even up to three-quarter pebbles are laid on the bottom of the bed for drainage, and can also be placed on top as a surface layer to prevent the sand being washed into furrows and even off the bed by the flow from the hose.

MANAGEMENT OF SAND CULTURE

The special requirements of sand culture can be grouped under two main headings:

1. Seed sowing and transplanting; and,
2. Solution application.

Raising plants. This is best done in ordinary seed boxes. Use fresh sand in each case, which obviates the need for sterilising. The same depth as with soil is used. The bottom of the box should be covered with fine gravel or glass wool to prevent sand draining through.

The seed is sown exactly as with soil, except that in most cases a more even covering is possible with sand, and therefore a lighter covering can be used.

Water the sand with hot or warm water a few hours before seed sowing in order to provide comfortable conditions for germination. After sowing the seed, sift *dry* sand on to the top. Wet sand is difficult to smooth evenly without disturbing the seed.

Cover with glass, or place in propagating frame in the ordinary way, and apply only water until the seed leaves show through. Then water with half-strength solution until ready for pricking or planting out. Most plants can be transplanted in an earlier stage from sand into the main sand beds or into soil, since the nature of the sand permits a free root run and the quicker establishment of a sufficient root system.

Except where the sand bed is required for other crops, and it would be a waste of space to keep it occupied for too long, it is usually better to seed directly into the bed in which it is intended to grow the plants.

This applies even to tomatoes and lettuce, which are usually "potted on" with soil. Even where tomatoes are germinated in boxes and potted singly, it is actually better to transplant them when about two and a half inches tall instead of waiting for the first flowers, as is usual in soil.

If plants are transplanted from sand to soil, keep as much sand on the roots as possible. If transplanting from soil to sand, it is usually better to wash off the soil.

With hardwood plants, however, such as roses, they appear to do better if a soil ball is left attached, although this should not be so large as to provide a permanent wet area round the roots.

Plants can also be raised very successfully in fine cinders, although in this case more careful attention to watering is required to prevent the seed-bed drying out.

Some growers advocate increasing the amount of phosphorous in the nutrient solution applied to seedlings and to plants when first transplanted, on the ground that this tends to increase root growth. I have tried this and found it beneficial in most cases. The recommended amount is 20 p.p.m. of phosphorous more than in the normal growing solution. The amount of phosphorous can be dropped to the proper level as soon as the plants are established.

Solution Application. The secret of this is to vary the feeding in accordance with what the plants require, not by any definite timetable. In the early days of soilless culture time-clocks and other devices were often used in order to provide a feed at fixed intervals. This was all very well in theory, but in practice feeding the same amount regardless of the weather often led to trouble. It soon came to be realised that Nature still knew best.

If the sand looks and feels dry, and the plants have the appearance of needing moisture, then is the time to apply the solution. If they appear quite happy, and the sand feels moist, leave them alone—even if it is quite a long time since they have been fed. It is not unusual for carnations in winter, for example, not to need watering or feeding for three weeks. On the other hand, tomato seedlings in summer may need watering twice a day.

On the same principle, giving quantities of liquid to

apply to stated areas of bed is not a great deal of use. It depends on so many factors not within the knowledge of the writer, that the best advice, even though it seems not very helpful, is really to urge the gardener or grower to learn to decide for himself. One greenhouse may need five gallons to a 100 square feet. Another may need twenty-five gallons. Sympathy with the plants and experience are the best guides.

One general principle holds good. The finer the sand, the more it retains moisture and the less often it will require watering. In addition, up to a depth of nine inches, the deeper the bed the greater can be the intervals between watering.

So far "watering" and applying nutrient solution have been referred to as the same operation. Actually, however, three different alternatives are possible:

1. Using freshly made solution for each watering;

2. Collection and re-use of solution for periods up to a fortnight; and

3. Alternate applications of solution and water.

The first method is the most popular. It means that chemicals have to be weighed out and mixed each time, but once these are worked out the actual weighing and mixing does not take long. No troubles through unbalanced solutions are likely to be encountered, and as already indicated, the cost of fertiliser grade chemicals is not such as to make the method too expensive.

The second method implies that the beds must be water-tight, and that means must be found for drainage to a central point and the construction of a sump to collect the solution. It also involves, of course, a pump to return the solution to the tank from which it is fed to the bed. In fact, if this method is used there seems no point in not going in for complete sub-irrigation by gravel culture, which is described in the next chapter.

The third method is often used, and indeed in summer when large amounts of moisture are required by some plants it is sometimes the better system. In general, however, the rapid changes in concentration resulting from going from solution to water and back again to solution do not provide the best conditions for roots to take up nutrients.

It is better, if it is felt that more water is required, to vary the dilution of the solution by giving a half or three-quarter strength feed. This has the same effect as alternate watering without the violent change in conditions.

Whichever method is used, however, it is wise to wash through the sand thoroughly every two months or so to leach out any excesses of chemicals remaining on the sand particles.

The more nearly the requirements of the plants approximate to the composition of the solution, the less often will this leaching be required. If, however, solution has been applied too often, or at too great a concentration, accumulations might make it advisable to leach more often. If growth appears to slow up, and there is no apparent reason, it is a wise precaution to leach and see if improvement takes place.

A few points regarding particular crops should be noted:

TOMATOES

Seed sowing. Sow in boxes in sand. Apply water only till germination.

Solution. The basic formula described in Chapter 3 adjusted to *pH* 6. Use at half-strength till planting out, when $2\frac{1}{2}$ inches tall. Sprinkle the solution between the rows in the box rather than on the plants. If the plants are two inches apart in the box, they can be planted out direct—otherwise they should be potted into 3-inch pots of sand and fed with half-strength solution, about $\frac{1}{4}$ pint of solution to each pot per day.

Planting out. Precisely as in soil. Distances should be the same as in soil. When planted out, apply solution gently round the base of the stem to settle the sand round the roots.

Growing on. Gradually increase the nitrogen to 300 p.p.m. and lower the potassium to 150, as outlined in Chapter 3.

LETTUCE

Seed sowing. Best done in rows or broadcast direct in the growing bed.

Solution. The basic formula can be used from the outset, but *it should be adjusted to pH* 7. Except in high summer, the concentration of the solution can be doubled if required and water applied alternately with solution.

Growing on. It is important, especially in dull cold weather, not to let the solution go on the leaves or round the stems of the lettuce. In small beds where the trouble would not be too great, applying solution through funnels so that it goes immediately below the level of the surface of the sand is often practised.

CARNATIONS

Propagation. As this is already usually done in beds of sand, even where it is intended to plant out in soil, this should present no difficulty. The only difference is that when using nutrient solution, it is applied at one-quarter strength as soon as the cuttings are rooted. The use of 10 per cent. more potassium in the solution than in the main growing beds hardens the cuttings up. Increasing the concentration has the same effect.

Planting out. Apply solution at half-strength to the beds the day before planting out. But if possible make it with *hot* water. This gives nice warm conditions for the young roots.

Solution. Use the basic formula, but with the nitrogen reduced to 100 and the potassium to 50 p.p.m. This is for young plants.

As the plants get older, increase to 130 N and 65 K. By the time they are three years old they can take 160 N and 80 K.

Growing on. In winter use a more concentrated solution applied less often—once in three weeks is often enough. In summer use a more dilute solution more often—perhaps once every four or five days, depending on the weather.

CUTTINGS

Cuttings root freely in sand culture. Even those that normally do well in compost often do better in nutrified sand.

Normally, a half-strength nutrient solution is used. Hormone solution can be used in the normal way before inserting the cuttings, and, thereafter, warm moist conditions maintained by the use of warmed nutrient solution.

OTHER CROPS

Because of the lack of obstruction to free root development, root crops do extraordinarily well in sand culture. Carrots, turnips, parsnips (which require a deep bed), beetroot, are among those often grown.

Any crops that can be grown in soil (not excluding trees) can be grown in sand.

9

GRAVEL CULTURE

IF you are one of those who like to see things work for themselves, then gravel culture will probably be your choice. It is the best method to make fully automatic. If required, an installation can be made to do all the watering, aeration, and feeding that plants need. In fact, if one of the latest devices which open and shut greenhouse ventilators thermostatically is installed as well, you have almost reached the stage when you can plant the crop, and then go away on holiday until it is time to come back and pick it!

Sub-irrigation of gravel beds is the nearest man has yet come to machine-made plants, and perhaps for this reason it has a peculiar fascination. You press a switch, a motor begins to hum, and the nutrient solution floods from below to feed the roots. It creeps up to the level you choose, an invisible switch comes into operation, and the solution flows silently out the unseen way it came. Out of your lifeless-looking bed of cinders or stones rises life in the form of flowers or fruit. And all you have done to achieve it is to move a finger!

Yes, the fascination is undeniable—but so are the drawbacks, too. It depends much on your own particular growing conditions and mental make-up which you think matters more—the "fors" or the "againsts".

GRAVEL CULTURE

Although usually called "gravel" culture, this type of growing includes all units which use solid media larger than sand. Pumice chippings, broken brick, vermiculite, cinders, granite chippings or crushed gravel, crushed clinker, and many other materials have been used. In all, the principle is the same—a watertight bed of some material in which the roots are embedded, fed by periodic flooding from below with nutrient solution.

The mechanical means by which this principle is carried out resolve themselves into two main groups:

1. Home and amateur installations; and,

2. Large scale and commercial installations.

HOME UNITS

BUCKET DESIGN. A box, metal tank, sink or any similar container is fitted with an outlet to take a hose. The other end of the hose is connected to a spout fitted to the side of a bucket near the bottom. When the bucket is raised above the level of the box, the solution flows down and into it; when the bucket is lowered again, the solution drains back again.

A piece of quarter or half-inch pipe can be bolted or soldered to the end of the box. With very small beds, glass tubing can be inserted in a cork, and the cork fitted into a hole in the end of the box.

Before deciding on a bucket, it is as well to fill one with water to the level you need and lift it several times to test the weight. If it is too heavy, you must use a smaller one. It is also wise to rig up a strong hook on which to hang the

100 SUCCESSFUL GARDENING WITHOUT SOIL

pail in the raised position. This hook should be as low as possible to ensure proper draining of the solution to the bed. Nine to twelve inches above the bed is enough. The lower the hook, the less effort is required.

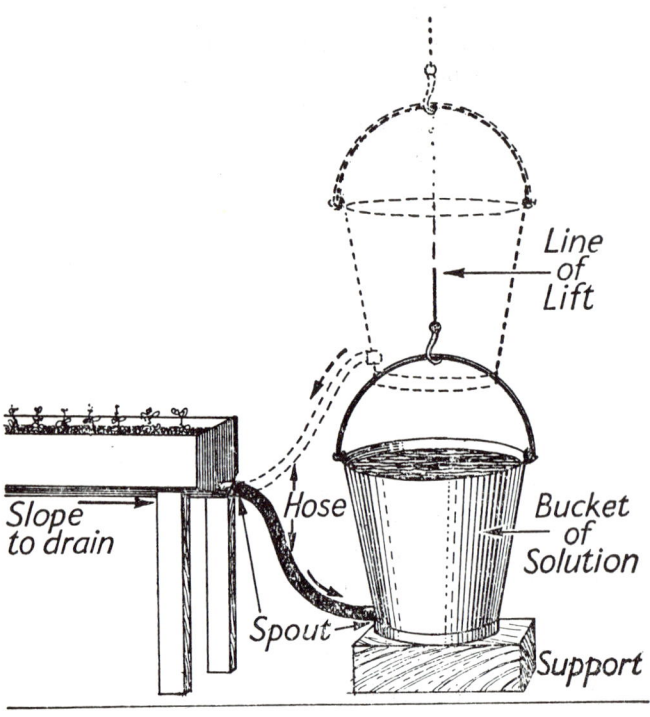

An alternative to using a smaller bucket is to rig up a hook and pulley. Then when raising the bucket, all that is necessary is to pull on the rope. With this method, of course, you must be very sure each time to fix the rope securely after lifting. A heavy bucket dropping on a bed of plants is the last thing they appreciate.

It is usually better to rig up a pulley for all pails of more then three gallons capacity. In practice it is difficult to obtain actual pails of that size, and steel drums or wooden barrels must be fitted with strong handles and used instead.

Twenty gallons is probably the most that could be recommended for pulley operation. Above that, however careful the operator, a suspended tank would become a danger to the gardener as well as the plants.

The size of bucket required can be worked out by measuring the bed and finding its volume. The capacity of the bucket must be at least half that volume. It has to be remembered that with buckets or tanks that are to be lifted, the useful level of filling is an inch or two below the top to avoid spilling.

As most buckets are galvanised, they should be coated with two coats of asphalte paint before use. If of enamel, they may be used as they are.

The boxes or containers used for the bed should be six to eight inches deep. If the solution container is large, several beds can be coupled together with rubber tubing and fed at the same time. The inlet pipe can be fitted at the end, at the side, or in the bottom. The position is not material so long as it allows for complete drainage. For this reason, if the pipe is in the side, the bottom of the inside bore should be a shade below the bottom of the container. Even though this makes it more awkward to fix, this is a necessary factor. The bed should have a slight downward slope to the outlet.

DIRECT FEED DESIGN

This is really a model of a set-up often seen on a commercial scale.

A bed is built of concrete, brick, wood or metal. Again the depth is at least eight inches.

The length for what can be fairly called "home" use rarely exceeds twenty feet. The width can be from one to four feet wide, but above that attention to plants in the centre becomes well-nigh impossible without damage to plants near the outside edge.

The bottom is sloped slightly to one end—the pipe end. Half an inch in ten feet is sufficient. It is also sloped either towards the centre in a shallow inverted V, or to one side. At the bottom of the slope a drainage channel is made, either round or angular. Above the channel are placed half-tiles, slates, black iron guttering, or wooden slats. *What* does not matter, so long as it allows a free flow beneath, prevents the gravel from falling into the channel, and does not adversely affect the plants.

At the drainage end, and again just below the lowest point, is fixed a pipe, protruding about six inches into the bed and under the channel cover. Three-quarter copper pipe is the correct size for most amateur installations.

In my experience the easiest way for the amateur to build a bed is to put up a wall of brick, faced inside with cement. Two bricks on edge give a depth of nine and a half inches, allowing for the cement. This depth allows for a one and a half inches slope from the sides of the bottom of the bed to the centre, and still leaves a good eight inches for the media. The bottom is best constructed by pouring in wet concrete, and then shaping with a wooden or metal mould specially made for the purpose. This is slid along the walls, keeping a constant height.

The drainage channel can be made at the same time by placing a piece of timber, or tiles in a line in the concrete, removing them when partial setting has taken place. The whole can then be finished off with a coating of pure waterproof cement, followed with two of asphalte paint.

There is more work in making such a bed than might be thought, but I have constructed several unaided and found them very satisfactory. The chief points to watch are that the slope of the bottom is even, leaving no depressions for pools to form, and that the cement facing is complete, excluding leaks.

One of the likeliest points for a leak is where the pipe enters the bottom of the bed. It is best to insert here a small black iron plate with a hole through which the pipe can be passed and screwed up with a nut on either side. This makes a watertight joint, and at the same time is able to take the strain of a hose being pulled about.

It is wise to bend a small piece of copper gauze over the end of the pipe in the bed to prevent any small particles of gravel being sucked into the pipe and blocking the pump.

The pump is best placed just alongside the solution tank. The intake is then short, and air leaks are not likely to develop. The tank can be on the ground and pump beside it, and the top of the pump must be at least six inches below the bottom of the bed, otherwise drainage will be difficult. One other provision is that the top of the pump must be below the lowest level to which the solution in the tank is likely to fall. If this is not done the pump will not be constantly primed. When switched on it may then race and eventually burn out—a great inconvenience and expense.

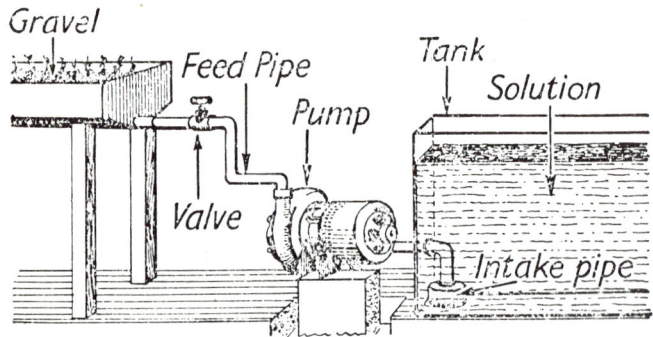

At the same time the pump should not be on the ground, since any water or solution may possibly leak into the mechanism and cause trouble. This is particularly vital if the water table in the ground on which the greenhouse is built is high.

Perhaps the best arrangement is for the tank to be half-sunk in the ground, and for the pump to be alongside it, standing on a wooden block, to which it can be screwed. The wooden block should itself stand in a miniature sump, so that any excess water will fall below the vital parts of the pump. Using a wooden base insulates the pump. A cement block could be used instead.

Although I have seen other types of pump recommended, the only type that I would myself consider using is the centrifugal type. This is simple, foolproof if properly installed, and allows the solution to flow through both ways. A small fountain-type pump with an outlet pipe for three-quarter or one-inch hose is sufficient for most amateur greenhouses. They can be bought,

GRAVEL CULTURE

.ogether with valve and strainer, and all necessary piping and joints for less than £10.

The inlet pipe for the pump is led into the bottom of the tank, through an elbow, ending on a brass or copper strainer. This is a cylinder of perforated metal. They are often sold with a foot valve incorporated, and it is as well to make sure that this can be unscrewed and dismantled before purchase. If the valve is left in when the pump is switched off the solution will not flow back again.

Automatic switching-off of the pump is best arranged by means of a mercury float switch in the tank. To buy a ready-made float switch means spending several pounds, but a competent electrician can make one up for a few shillings. It should be properly earthed, as it is operating so near to water, and should be so arranged that it cuts out the motor when the solution level in the bed reaches one inch below the top of the gravel. It may require some adjustment to see that the switch does not cut in again before the bed has completely drained.

A gate-valve should be fitted between the pump and the bed so that if necessary the solution can be kept in the bed. This is useful for planting out, and for using a sterilising solution occasionally. If more than one bed is being pumped from the same tank, a valve should be included at the end of each bed.

The volume of tank required must be worked at in the same way as for the smaller home units. Find the volume of bed or beds to be filled, and then utilise a tank of half that capacity. If it is more than half, so much the better. But it should not be less. Second-hand metal tanks of 30, 50 and up to 250 gallon capacity are come by quite easily. Although no longer serviceable for water supplies, rubbed down with steel wool and coated with asphalte they are capable of giving years more service for gardening purposes.

Control of Pumping

Such a unit as the one described works in this way: When switched on, the pump draws the solution up through the pipe into the bed, when it flows along the channel the full length of the gravel.

Then it begins to rise, percolating between the particles of gravel and pushing up the air with it. At the appointed height the pump cuts out, and the solution slowly drains back again through the pump into the tank. At the same time air is drawn into the bed. The roots are then left in a saturated, aerated atmosphere until the next pumping. During this time the air in the moisture film (which is actually nutrient solution) on the particles gets less and the film itself becomes more concentrated as it evaporates and as the roots take up nutrients. The pumping must be so arranged, therefore, that before the solution film has dried up too much, the next pumping renews it. This interval depends on the plant, the stage of its growth, the size and physical nature of the gravel, the weather, the depth of the bed, and several other factors. It may vary from three or four pumpings a day for tomatoes in summer, to one a week for carnations in winter. There can be no hard and fast rule, and the only real guide is experience. But it is surprising how little of this a genuine gardener needs when he takes up soilless culture. A good grower can tell a happy plant whether it is in soil or stones.

It will be seen, therefore, that any automatic system

for pumping turns what should be a variable factor into a fixed one. When we say automatic feeding, we really mean feeding by time-clock. Various ingenious methods for this kind of feeding have been tried, including drip and ball valves, but the only really reliable one is the time-switch. To use this you set the switch to work every twelve hours, or four hours, or whatever you decide.

But it is obvious that if you set the clock for three pumpings every twenty-four hours in bright hot weather, and then the weather turns dull and cool, the plants are going to be over-fed. And similarly if dull weather turns hot. You can compromise by striking the "happy medium" but this means that you will be wrong all the time, even though to a lesser extent.

So by and large I do not recommend time-switches in the ordinary way. The only valid use for them is for the amateur who *must* be away all day or for days on end and who has no one else to switch on for him. In such a case a greenhouse that will go on working while its owner is about his business is something that he could get in no other way.

Management of Solution

The solution, on an average, takes about three times as long to drain completely back into the tank as it takes to pump up. That is, if it takes half an hour to flood up to the pre-arranged level, it will take an hour and a half to flow back. The quicker this process takes place the better the aeration and the better the growth of many crops. The pumping, however, must not be so violent as to damage the roots either by direct agitation or by chafing between gravel particles. It is to avoid this that the channel is included to direct the force of the flow first along the bottom of the bed. If the size of pump is small the speed of drainage can be improved by including a second pipe at the tank end which can be opened when pumping is complete, and thus provide two drainage outlets.

This, of course, is led back into the tank. It is actually an advantage to have this second pipe partly open during the pumping. Part of the solution will then flow directly back into the tank, and if a fall is arranged between the end of the pipe and the top of the solution, the liquid will dissolve a certain amount of air as it returns. This will increase the time taken to pump to the required level, but will often improve growth.

Some of the solution will always be used up during pumping, by direct uptake into the roots, by the solution film left on the particles, and by evaporation. In hot weather during periods of full growth, this can be as much as 30 per cent. of the total volume per day. It is for this reason that it is wise to have a tank that is too big rather than one that is too small. The bigger the solution volume, the less will be the loss of water and the less the change of composition of the solution. This water loss can be made up in the ways already described—either by making up to the original level each day, or by going from too great a volume to too small a volume over a period of days. It is important, however, to make up the level when the tank is completely drained. Even when actual flowing back has stopped, considerable drippage will still go on which can add materially to the volume of solution in the tank. When taking the *pH* of the solution to adjust to the required level the sample should be taken after pumping, preferably just before another pumping is due.

The merits and demerits of changing the solution completely or testing for additions of nutrient have already been discussed, but if samples are taken for chemical testing, they should also be taken just before a pumping is due.

THE GRAVEL

Various types of media have already been discussed. The most easily obtained, one of the cheapest, and one of the most satisfactory for general growth is cinders or crushed clinker. They must, however, be well weathered for six months or so by being left out in the open. Occasionally they are acid or alkaline in reaction, but a weathering of this kind seldom fails to reduce them to as near the neutral point as is required.

Pumice chippings are even more suitable. They are invariably chemically inert and require no pretreatment. They are very retentive of moisture, soft enough not to damage roots, and hard enough not to disintegrate easily. They are, however, expensive. For the amateur they offer the prospect of a clean, white, attractive-looking bed, but on a commercial scale they cannot be recommended.

I have never tried broken brick, but have heard of it being successfully used.

Vermiculite, unless mixed with a large proportion of sand or gravel, is hardly suitable for sub-irrigation, as it is too light and too retentive of moisture. It is excellent for rooting cuttings and young seedlings, but it disintegrates rather readily and is also difficult to remove from the roots. A good deal is therefore lost when transplanting.

All these porous types of media, however, suffer in the

long run from the disadvantage already indicated in the chapter on water culture.

This is that over a period of years they acquire on their inner surfaces amounts of the nutrient elements which, by becoming available to the roots, may throw the solution out of balance.

Many people appear to have used cinders and the like for a number of years without trouble. Others report difficulties after only a year or so. It seems to depend on the circumstances. Enough information is to hand, however, to make it possible to say that on an average, after three years, troublesome accumulations are possible.

Gravel, on the other hand, has no inner surfaces as have porous media. There is only the one surface—the outside one. And experience indicates that by leaching with water, acidified with sulphuric acid to pH 4, it is possible satisfactorily to clear away all except a negligible quantity of anything that is adsorbed. With porous media, on the other hand, as much as fifty washings have been undertaken without completely 'inertialising' the media.

Yet gravel itself is not so satisfactory a medium for several reasons, the principal ones being that it is not so retentive of moisture, and that it offers a chilling atmosphere for roots as against the warmer atmosphere in porous media.

Here is a pretty problem. What is the answer? There are several possibilities:

Analysing the media. The pioneer in this technique is Mr. W. Doxford, of Sussex, who has worked for a number of years to perfect a system of analysing the cinders, finding out what they contain, estimating how much is available to the roots, and making an allowance for this in the composition of the solution.

Although the results of this system have not at the time of writing been sufficiently established to make public, there is no doubt that the crops on which experiments have been conducted for ten years or more have been outstandingly successful. I have myself followed the system for cinder cultivation of tomatoes and found it to be productive of remarkable results.

It is with regret, therefore, that I must add my considered opinion that except for the chemist or the chemically-minded amateur, whose enthusiasm allows him to ignore costs, it is not practicable.

Think what it means. First, you have to analyse the solution weekly. That alone is a forbidding task to one not versed in chemistry, and perhaps not very interested. Then you have to take what is called an extract from the cinders, and put this extract itself through precisely the same tests. Then, based on experience and records, you must arbitrarily decide how much of what you find in the cinders is likely to be available to the roots. This may vary from 20 to 80 per cent. of each element. Then you calculate how much you have to add to replace nutrients taken up by the plants, less what they may be able to take from the cinders.

These tests and calculations become easier with practice, but most people attempting soilless culture, if faced with such a task, would come to the conclusion that it would be better to return to soil culture.

Replacing the media. This is the most practical method for the amateur. After all, his beds may give no trouble for many years. And if they do, it is inconvenient, but not a herculean task, to take out all the old cinders and replace with new every three or four years.

Using non-porous types of media. This is the commercial man's answer. Despite the advantages of porous media under certain conditions, on a large scale it is safer to rely on gravel. It is easily obtained, graded for size, and fairly easily cleaned. It does not tend to break up and clog the drainage and pumps. It is easily sterilised.

MEDIA CHARACTERISTICS

Size of media. An aggregate for sub-irrigation must be properly screened. If this is not done, either the particles will be too large and allow the roots to dry out, or they will be too fine, and clog the system.

A good average size for an aggregate is between one-sixteenth inch and three-eighths inch for gravel, and between one-eighth and half-inch for porous media such as cinders or pumice.

Cinders which are soft and tend to disintegrate are not really suitable, as they wear down in use and the resulting powder clogs in the channel and pump. On the other hand, hard, sharp gravel or chippings may cut the roots and stems. Besides the actual damage, disease organisms may enter the wounds and cause trouble.

Chemical nature of media. It must not be forgotten that gravel may exhibit the same calcareous nature as the sand already described in the last chapter. The same tests should therefore be made, and the same treatment given. As the gravel will be in watertight beds, however, it is possible in this case to pump in the phosphate solution and leave it in for twenty-four hours or so for the reaction to be given full scope.

Besides the calcium in calcareous gravel, sometimes magnesium may be found as well. In this case a sample should be analysed or sent for analysis. In the event of 10 or more parts per million being found, allowance should be made for this amount in calculating the formula. This means that only 40 or less parts per million of magnesium are required. Similarly, little or no calcium need be used in the formula, as the roots will obtain sufficient for growth from the particles with which they are in contact. If superphosphate is used as the source of phosphorous, this will inevitably add a certain amount of calcium sulphate. For this reason monocalcium phosphate, which contains a much smaller proportion of calcium, is to be preferred in dealing with gravels of this type. Special attention must be paid to the amount of phosphorous in the solution, as if this is allowed to fall, the gravel particles will lose their phosphate coating and the calcium will again become exposed, resulting in an alkaline solution.

Some types of media, notably cinders, are acid in reaction, and benefit from a treatment with a 5 per cent. solution of sodium hydroxide, which is left to soak in the same way as the phosphate solution. Before treating them, however, they should be thoroughly leached first with ordinary water, as in many cases this alone is sufficient to wash away the alkalies. Two soakings of twenty-four hours are usually sufficient.

After treatment of any kind, the media should be given a thorough washing with plain water.

Often the gravel or cinders are dirty, and require washing. This is best done with a hose applied at as great a pressure as can be arranged.

This washing should preferably not be done in the bed, since if there is a good deal of clayey, silty material, this will wash down and clog the drainage. It is better to do it on an open space with a concrete or brick floor. It is remarkable how much dirt apparently clean gravel can hold. The only media which I have found to be invariably clean is pumice, and even that contains a good deal of dust.

Prevention of Algae. It has already been stated that the solution level should not be allowed to penetrate into the top inch of the bed. This is to prevent the growth of algae, the green scum which robs the roots of oxygen, makes an unpleasant smell, and gives the beds an unpleasant appearance.

As a further precaution, beds may be finished off with a layer of "three-quarter down" pebbles, which should effectively prevent any algae.

I have dealt in detail with this direct-feed system, since it is probably the best form of soilless culture for the busy man whose greenhouse must not be allowed to take up too much of his time, and also because it illustrates the principle of any form of sub-irrigation. I have tried to be as helpful as possible in practical details, since it is usually in these that the average grower meets with difficulty.

COMMERCIAL UNITS

Commercial units can be considered under three headings:

1. Direct feed units;

2. Gravity feed units; and

3. Flume, or open channel systems.

The first of these is simply the larger version of what has already been described in detail for the small greenhouse. Only an outline of such installations can be given.

Commercial Direct Feed Units

Principle. As in small greenhouses.

Construction. The tank containing the solution is usually of reinforced concrete, with the inlet pipe either at one end of the beds or beneath them, in the centre. When a number of beds are pumped from the same tank, a manifold is constructed to equalise the pressure of the supply. The longest length of bed is usually 100 feet, and ten such beds are often operated as one unit, fed either from one very large tank or from several smaller ones. Water engineers should be consulted as to the correct size of pump and piping. Valves are fitted at the end of each bed to make final adjustments in pressure. It is important that all the beds should fill evenly, otherwise some beds may be undernourished and others receive too much.

For this type of installation, levels are vital. Each bed must be the same height as the others, and the fall to the drainage end must be the same in each case.

Usually an electric pump is used to provide power, but it is wise to have a petrol engine stand-by in case of power or motor failure.

Gravity Units

Principle. When a large number of beds are being operated, the cost of pumping and the time taken are a material item. The gravity feed unit reduces this considerably.

Construction. Beds are arranged in series, usually of three, one below the other. The solution is contained in a tank raised above the top end of the uppermost bed.

It flows by gravity into the bottom of the top bed, until it reaches the correct level, when an automatic syphon comes into play and the solution flows down into the bottom of the second bed, and so on to the third and lowest bed. Each succeeding bed is shorter, so that although solution is lost through uptake and evaporation in the bed above, there is still enough for the bed below. In the larger American units the upper bed is 120 feet long, the middle one 100 feet, and the bottom one 80 feet.

At the bottom of the installation the solution flows out into a drainage channel and sump, from which it is pumped back again into the gravity tank ready for the next feed. As there is usually several hours before this operation, the size of the pump and pipe required is much less than would be needed in a direct-feed system of equal size.

Flume System

Principle. Flume systems can be either gravity-fed or direct-fed, but in either case the solution flows to the beds through an open ditch or channel known as a flume. The advantage is that there is a minimum of piping and that the solution is more aerated than when it flows through pipes. In addition there is no need for the terracing required for gravity-fed units.

Construction. Usually there is a large overhead tank in the centre of the installation. From this the solution flows into a lock with wooden gates opening on either side, one lower than the other. The lower gate is kept closed and the solution flows out of one side of the lock to feed the series of beds on one side. The solution enters through holes or short lengths of pipe at the end of each bed.

When it reaches the required level, the lower lock gate is opened and the solution flows down to the lower beds. When these in turn are fed, a third gate is opened and the solution falls into a sump from which it is pumped back into the tank again.

To construct such large systems as these is an engineering contract. Details can be found in a number of American works, and space forbids any attempt to give here all the dimensions and instructions required. Certain details, however, are the same whatever the size of the unit, and are of interest to all who take up sub-irrigation culture even on a small scale.

Beds. The only materials now generally recommended are concrete and asphalte-sand mastic. Metal, wood, asbestos cement, and several other materials have not been found entirely satisfactory for various reasons.

Concrete beds have reinforced sides and bottoms, and are $1\frac{1}{2}$ to 2 inches thick. An expansion joint of copper or asphalte every ten feet is advisable to prevent cracking due to changes of temperature. The inner surface is coated with hot mopped asphalte or with asphalte paint.

The asphalte-sand mix consists of 70 per cent. clean *dry* sand and 30 per cent. asphalte. They are mixed hot and poured into the forms just as is concrete.

Whatever the length of the bed, it should not be more than four feet wide, and should be deep enough to allow for at least six inches of media. In long beds a slope up to two inches per 100 feet for drainage is recommended. The cross-wise slope either to one side or to the centre should be one inch.

Drainage. Tile or asbestos half-round guttering is the most suitable material for the drainage channel in the beds. It is more practical to have this channel at one side, since if there is any question of clogging it is easier to expose and clear without disturbing the crop. Galvanised guttering, although often recommended, is not thoroughly suitable since even two coats of asphalte is not always enough to prevent damage from the zinc.

One of the most practical channels I have seen is that developed by Mr. J. W. Godber, of Cornwall. In this case an inner wall of asbestos board is placed along one side of the bed, kept in position by the weight of the media pressing against it. Wood blocks at intervals keep it an even distance from the side of the bed. There is thus an open channel about one inch wide. This type of channel gives more aeration, and is also very easy to keep clean and free from roots.

All drainage tiles should be kept in short lengths. This allows easier access for the solution from the channel to the bed. If the bottom of the bed is left fairly rough, the tile will virtually rest on miniature corrugations, and the solution will be able to ebb and flow easily between the bottom of the tile and the bottom of the bed. If the bottom is smooth, small pieces of slate or wood must be placed in position so as to leave a space. This gap, however, should not be so large as to allow the media to make its way into the channel and cause blockage. Glass wool or copper gauze can be used to block any gaps that are too large.

Tanks. Steel is the most suitable material for the storage tanks. It should be coated first with neat cement, and then two coats of asphalte.

If steel is not available, reinforced concrete is also used. As the volume of the tank should be up to twice the amount of solution required to flood the beds, the cost is a big item. For this reason many growers favour overhead tanks rather than face the cost of excavation to contain a tank holding many thousand of gallons.

Pumps and piping. As the nutrient solution is always slightly acid, certain metals, chiefly zinc, dissolve readily enough to poison the plant. I have had a whole crop of tomatoes affected by one iron hook dissolving because it was in contact with a copper wire in the solution. Copper alone is fairly safe, and tin and aluminium appear entirely safe unless the *pH* is very low.

What actually happens when two metals are present is that (with the nutrient solution) they form an electric cell. With zinc and iron, for example, the zinc dissolves and the iron does not. With copper and iron, the iron dissolves, as does lead. Steel is quite safe. Bronze is reasonable in small quantity, but not brass, as it contains zinc.

SEED SOWING IN GRAVEL

Certain types of seed may be sown direct in gravel, particularly the larger seeds, such as peas and beans. To do this satisfactorily, however, the media should be one-eighth to three-eighths inch in particle size, not larger, as may be used for general growth. Smaller seed such as carrot can be successfully sown if a mulch of sand is scattered over the surface of the gravel. This should be kept as shallow as possible in order to prevent the gravel from being clogged with the sand, which will gradually wash down.

Plants which are normally potted up before planting out, such as tomatoes, are very successfully grown in pots or boxes of fine cinders. One-eighth to three-eighths of an inch in size is ideal. The seed is sown in the ordinary way, three to a three-inch pot, and kept moist. It should be watered once each day. When showing through, half-strength solution is applied. Such seedlings grow very rapidly and transplant very well. Fresh cinders should be used each time, however.

Sterilisation. Gravel is much easier to sterilise than soil, and a good deal easier than cinders or pumice. A number of chemicals, some of them very poisonous, have been developed for this purpose, but for the ordinary gardener it is best to keep to formaldehyde.

The strength to use is a 7,500 p.p.m. concentration of commercial formalin (40 per cent. formaldehyde) or a 1:100 dilution. This should be pumped into the bed and left for at least twelve hours. At the same time the beds should be covered with canvas, roofing paper, or sacks to keep in the fumes.

It is quite in order to pump one bed at a time, back into the tank, then the next bed, and so on. This reduces the amount of formalin required.

After sterilising, the aggregate should be thoroughly leached with plain water several times. With a porous aggregate three washings might be required. A precaution when handling concentrated formalin is to use rubber gloves, apron and a gas mask.

It is quite safe to sterilise a bed next to one containing growing plants.

Solution temperature. Although it is seldom economical or even beneficial to warm it more than 5 degrees above the temperature of the night air in the greenhouse, the temperature of the solution should not be allowed to fall below that of the air. The most practical method of achieving this is to have the solution tank standing on the ground in the house, where it is surrounded by the air. If the tank is below ground, a small steam or hot water coil can bring it up to the required temperature.

Electric heating cables and immersion heaters are usually dangerous to use because of corrosion, unless they are of a special acid-proof type.

A good many crops, notably tomatoes, benefit from bottom heat. The way to do this is not to instal heating cables in the aggregate iself. The heat from these is too high and too near the roots to be suitable. The best way, if practicable, is to build raised beds and run the heating pipes underneath them.

10

COMMERCIAL SOILLESS CULTURE

COMMERCIAL growers are naturally a hard-headed lot. They need a lot of convincing, and, so far, it must be admitted, very few of them have been convinced that soilless culture is a good thing.

The reasons are not far to seek. Costs of greenhouse growing have mounted to such high levels since the war that where we used to reckon in hundreds of pounds, we must now go up to thousands. Even with soil culture, a grower on a big scale can lose thousands on one crop if anything important goes wrong. Why, then, should he add to his already serious commitments the further risk of growing by a method with which he is not familiar and in which he might fail?

It has been proved—and I mean scientifically, horticulturally, and definitely proved—by Mr. S. R. Mullard and others that soilless culture is capable of giving a bigger yield than soil, and a more uniform one. Yet, because of the high cost of installation and the understandable reticence of the successful soil grower, that proof has passed more or less unheeded in the trade.

Yet soilless culture *is* a commercial proposition. Once its principles and practice are thoroughly grasped, the pitfalls are no more than are always being encountered with soil. And once success is achieved, that success is usually greater than with soil.

I do not mean that there is a fortune awaiting anyone

who tries it. Even if success is immediate, and continuous, it has been estimated that it takes at least five years to get back the initial outlay on a sub-irrigation installation. But as in any other human endeavour, there are good rewards for good work.

I have often been asked for advice on starting soilless culture on a commercial scale, and I give it with diffidence because I am myself an amateur. It is this. Be sure, first, to undertake trials for several years with a small installation. If you already have a nursery, try one house, or one bed. If you are just starting, start with soil and move over to sand or gravel gradually. Then, when lessons have been learned and confidence gained, you can take the more ambitious step of running an entirely soilless nursery.

I have assumed so far that you are interested in soilless culture and want to try it. But suppose you are either indifferent or antagonistic. Is it worth your while even thinking about it?

I suggest it is, and for these reasons:

1. Labour costs are reduced, especially on digging, soil changing, watering, weeding and sterilising.
2. The growth is more uniform, and more easily and quickly controlled.
3. The quality of the soil is immaterial. Your site can be anywhere conditions are good.
4. Yields are as good as the best soil yields.
5. A number of diseases, particularly soil-borne ones, are virtually eliminated.
6. There is no better way of learning what plants need. It is possible to learn immediately and certainly the effects of variation in any of the elements, as well as of the oxygen supply and concentration of nutrients.

HIGHER COST

Against these factors must be weighed the fact that except for sand culture, all forms of soilless culture are more expensive to instal than normal soil beds. Watertight beds, pumps, tanks, piping, valves and control gear have today reached prices that need the most serious consideration before they are paid. It is true that once bought they last for many years without further expense. It is also true that maintenance costs are very low compared with up-to-date methods of soil culture. But even allowing for these factors the initial cost must be weighed in coming to any decision.

Perhaps the second most important consideration in the balance against soilless culture is that despite many writings to the contrary, some form of informed—I hesitate to use the word "expert"—supervision is necessary. A good many problems may arise, and if money depends on their prompt and satisfactory solution, the answers must be found quickly and certainly.

Some of these problems I have already tried to deal with in this book. Others will be considered in a later chapter. But inevitably there will occur technical and practical considerations that only a study of the conditions on the spot will resolve.

This does not mean that a highly-qualified scientist or consultant must be called in. Provided the grower has adopted the suggestion of gaining experience on a small scale before he undertakes a big venture, he himself will be able to solve most of his problems. A little chemical knowledge, a good deal of ordinary common sense and a keen sympathy for and observation of the plants, will do the rest.

Unfortunately no complete account of costs and returns of any soilless culture nursery run on a commercial basis are available for publication. All that can be done is to point to a number of installations that have been profitably run for a number of years, with the obvious comment that if they can do it, others can.

A PRACTICAL INSTALLATION

One of the most practically-run commercial nurseries in the British Isles is that of Mr. J. Richmond, of Peel, near Blackpool. Mr. Richmond has 15,000 square feet of carnations in sand.

His houses are laid out in beds 100 feet long by 4 feet 3 inches wide, built of bricks placed sideways on with half-inch gaps left in the bottom row for drainage. The base of the bed is made of cement raised one inch in the middle so as to divert seepings to either side, and thence through the slits in the brick on to the walks.

To prevent the sand in the beds from seeping out through the slits, half to three-quarter inch stones are placed over the bottom and sides of the bed. This, he decided, was a better form of drainage than a drain along the centre, which is too difficult to clear if it becomes choked.

Here follows Mr. Richmond's own description of his lay-out and methods:

> There is no need to coat the beds with asphalte as often recommended. In fact, this results in them remaining too wet. Despite what I have read in books, I have never experienced any trouble from the roots coming into contact with the untreated cement.

Solution is applied from two 400-gallon tanks. The main feed pipe is taken from each tank to the centre of the houses, where it branches laterally across, over each bed being a valve. This enables hoses to be clipped on to each valve and avoids having to drag the pipe over large distances. The minor elements I make up separately in a 40-gallon tank, at such a strength as to need one gallon of minor concentrate per 400 gallons of major solution.

On top of the sand in the beds is a layer of pebbles, which enables feeding to be done at full strength without washing holes in the sand. The rate is 300 gallons an hour through three-quarter inch hose.

Planting distance is determined partly through the requirements of each variety, but chiefly through the result desired—quality or quantity. I use the happy medium—eight inches between plants, and seven to ten between rows.

After planting out I feed with half-strength solution until the plants are established.

More plants are killed by too much watering than by too little. I feed every five days in summer, and up to once a fortnight or even longer in winter. The aim is to keep on the dry side, so that the roots really have to go searching. When you do water, make the beds really wet. In my case I give 300 gallons per house.

Solutions

For young plants, I use:

> 120 p.p.m. N sodium nitrate.
> 50 K potassium sulphate.
> 50 P superphosphate.
> 50 Mg magnesium sulphate.

Trace Elements.

5 p.p.m. *Fe* Ferric ammonium citrate	38 oz.
1 *B.* Boric acid	7·2 oz.
1 *Mn* manganese sulphate	5·2 oz.

This is dissolved in 20 gallons of water, and one gallon of the concentrate added to each 400 gallons of main solution.

As the plants get older, I alter to 135 N and 63 K. Above this I find the plants begin to harden.

By the time the plants are three years old they will take the full balance, which is 155 N to 80 K.

If there is one thing that I have learned, it is this—listen to the story the plants themselves tell you, and you will not go far wrong. How plants will grow on some of the highly-concentrated formulæ you see advertised especially in American books, is more than I can fathom. In my experience, and that of many with whom I have come in contact, the lower the concentration, in general, the better the growth.

The same lesson applies to feeding—give solution when the feel of the sand tells that it is right. Regular feeds at calculated intervals are wrong.

There are three guides to feeding:

1. The appearance of the plants.

2. The type of weather.

3. The required concentration.

In summer, with rapid drying of the beds, a weaker solution, applied more often, is the rule. In winter, when beds remain wet longer, a more concentrated solution applied less often is best. Low concentration makes growth more succulent, and a higher concentration harder.

The cost of chemicals amounts to 3s. 4d. a week—cheap enough, in all conscience.

Some of Mr. Richmond's beds have included in them a proportion of about one-tenth soil, and this, in his opinion, improves growth slightly.

The cost of the installation, including the brick beds, was (in 1948) £100 per 100 foot house of four beds.

Another interesting factor was that the tanks in which the solution was mixed were galvanised iron, entirely unpainted, and yet no trouble was experienced from zinc toxicity.

Successful crops of tomatoes and lettuce have been grown in the same beds.

SAND SUB-IRRIGATION

The nursery of Mr. J. W. Godber at Perranporth, Cornwall, is unusual in that it combines both sub-irrigation and sand culture. There are two nurseries, one with just under half an acre under glass and the other a short distance away including one of the biggest of the new alloy greenhouses.

The concrete tanks are four feet wide with the bottom sloping about one inch to the middle, or in some cases to one side. On the bottom is placed about two inches of coarse aggregate, which is also arranged up the sides. The centre is filled with sand. Both aggregate and sand are different grades of a local product of the China clay industry which is ideal for the purpose but would be uneconomical to transport to other parts of the country.

Either in the centre or at one side are inserted pieces of asbestos board cut the same depth as the bed, forming a channel about an inch wide, the asbestos being held at this distance with wood blocks. This channel is also filled with the coarse medium. The beds have a fall to one end, and an outlet there allows for drainage.

The solution is mixed in a 2,000 gallon tank situated at the highest point in the nursery, and fed through a two-inch gravity main and one-inch delivery pipe to copper pipes which actually feed the beds. When two pipes feed one bed, they are half-inch. When one pipe is used, it is three-quarter inch.

A small pump assists the gravity feed and helps to equalise the feed pressure. The solution actually reaches the beds through perforations in the copper piping, one-sixteenth inch in diameter and about nine inches apart.

In order to prevent blockage of these holes, a filter of one-thirty-second inch mesh is placed at the beginning of the gravity main.

The solution flows through the pipe perforations, down into the channel of coarse sand, to the bottom of the bed.

From there it begins to flow down the bed towards the drainage outlet, but at the same time upwards through the sand by capillary action. Feeding stops as soon as solution is seen to begin coming out of the drainage outlet.

Both carnations and tomatoes are grown by the same method, although a number of the tomatoes are in separate pots. The sand for the tomatoes is leached with water once a week, and that for the carnations once a month. The sand for the tomatoes is sterilised with formalin each year, and a proportion renewed at the same time.

The formula for the tomatoes at the time of obtaining my information contained 140 N and 325 K, and feeding was three times a day in summer. Boron, manganese and iron are fed, but not copper or zinc.

Feeding for the carnations is every three or four days in summer and about once a fortnight in winter.

No definite figures for present day costs of chemicals are available, but when a check was made a year or two ago, it amounted to only a few shillings a week. For this reason no attempt is made to collect and re-use the solution.

FLOWERS IN GRAVEL

The nursery of Messrs. Foxwells Ltd., at Balcombe in Sussex includes 8,000 square feet of gravel beds for the cropping of tomatoes, lettuce, sweet-peas and zinnias. The gravel is one-eighth to three-eighths, fed by gravity and sub-irrigation.

This is an example of the successful operation of a unit using the same solution continuously, replenishing by testing the solution and making up the salts as indicated.

Feeding varies from three times daily in summer to three times weekly in winter, and chemical tests for the main elements are made weekly in summer and fortnightly in winter.

The whole installation is operated from one 5,000 gallon reservoir situated in a building adjoining the greenhouse, and unheated.

An interesting feature at this nursery is a 675 square feet sand bed used mainly for raising plants for the larger gravel installation. Cornish sand is also used in this bed, fed by sub-irrigation and gravity. In this case trouble was experienced in securing uniformity of growth, as those plants near the source of nutrient supply developed better than those farther away.

THE FLUME SYSTEM

A feature of the carnation nursery of Messrs. A. G. Sparkes near Littlehampton, in Sussex, is what amounts virtually to the flume system.

Solution is mixed in a large underground tank, and fed by pumping up into a concrete channel running alongside the beds. Through access holes in the sides of the beds it flows in and up to a pre-arranged level.

The beds are of concrete, filled with gravel of the usual size for the purpose. Exceptionally good growth has been obtained, and this is attributed partly to the good aeration of the solution ensured through the very rapid pumping and open flow through the channels.

A number of commercial nurseries are operating in the United States, chiefly on the gravel sub-irrigation method. One of the first was the George J. Ball Incorporated concern at West Chicago, Illinois, where more than ten years' experience has been gained. About 6,000 feet of beds are used to grow sweet-peas, carnations, stocks, snapdragons, and chrysanthemums.

Messrs. J. L. Dillon of Bloomsburg, Pennsylvania, grow roses successfully in gravel. Mr. Ross Churchward, of Columbia, Ohio, is a very prominent grower of carnations in gravel. An interesting feature of his work is that after keeping careful records he is able to report that labour costs in production have been cut by half compared with soil culture.

Another of the pioneers in soilless culture, beginning as early as 1936, are Messrs. Yoder Brothers of Barberton, Ohio. Messrs. J. W. Davis, of Terre Haute, Indiana, were also early in the field, and are still active.

Many other firms operate successfully in the U.S.A. After the war there was a considerable increase in this form of culture in tropical and semi-tropical climates, such as Florida, Puerto Rico, and islands in the Caribbean. One of the most recent and successful was Modern Farms in Florida.

There are, of course, many other concerns in many other parts of the world. No attempt at a comprehensive survey has been made. But enough has been said, surely, to indicate that, properly undertaken, soilless culture is a commercial proposition.

DIFFERENT PROBLEMS

Anyone contemplating starting a soilless culture nursery, however, should, before starting, consider very carefully how his problems differ from those of the man thinking only in terms of soil.

First is the question of the site. It has already been stated that the quality of the soil is immaterial. The availability of the right kind of sand or cinders or whatever is being used, is, however, definitely not. Sand or other aggregate should be available at between fifteen and twenty shillings per ton delivered, if it is to be an economic proposition. Similarly, water of a kind capable of being used without detriment $MUST$ be to hand.

All nurseries, of whatever type, are more costly to lay out if the land has a considerable slope. In soilless culture, however it is possible to make effective use of a slope for gravity feeding, particularly in the terrace system. It must not be forgotten, though, that if extensive levelling has to be done it is an expensive business.

Next, the plan of the nursery must be thought out from a different point of view. There must be the propagation beds, the main growing beds, the tanks and heating system, and the service buildings.

The tanks and flow systems should be so arranged as to minimise the length of piping, and also so that the pump is situated in the place where it will work with most efficiency. The tank, or tanks, must be so situated that they are not exposed to chilling winds or the entry of dirt and disease. They should be fairly close to a supply of hot water if the chill has to be taken off before pumping. At the same time, the reservoirs must not be so much in the way as to hinder cultivation or take up valuable growing space unnecessarily. If concrete is used, once constructed, a large reservoir is very difficult to alter, so that its position must be very carefully thought out in advance. This applies to the possibility of future development as well as to immediate needs.

The service buildings must include a chemical storage room, where the salts used can be kept dry and ready for use. This room must be kept exclusively for the chemicals, and not used to store tools in addition, as the fumes from some chemicals will quickly tarnish and corrode them.

If the regular testing of nutrient solutions is to be undertaken, then there must be a laboratory fitted with hot and cold water, and with a north window.

Electricity should be available for driving pumps, and a petrol pump kept as a stand-by in case of electricity or pump failure.

Working on a large scale naturally introduces problems which do not trouble the amateur. One of the inevitable ones is the ordering of chemicals in quantity. It is hardly possible to calculate to fine limits how much might be required, but the following amounts recorded by the Unites States Army Air Force hydroponic department may be of assistance. They give the amount of chemicals required for one years's operation of a soilless culture installation of 10,000 square feet:

Chemicals	Weight n Pounds
Potassium Nitrate	5,000
Magnesium suphate	4,000
Monocalcium phosphate	4,000
Calcium sulphate	4,000
Calcium nitrate	5,000
Potassium sulphate	5,000
Sodium nitrate	4,000
Ferrous sulphate	200
Manganese sulphate	200
Boric Acid	10
Copper sulphate, and Zinc sulphate	5
Sulphuric acid	300
Potassium hydroxide	25
Formalin (for sterilising)	3,000
Water	600,000 (U.S.) gallons

The amounts depend, of course, on what formula is being used, what crop is being grown, whether the solution is allowed to flow away to waste, and so on. But the weights are at least some indication of what might be required.

SPECIAL METHODS

The mixing and application of the nutrient solution is treated slightly differently on a big scale. In the first place, in direct systems, it is usual to have a "mixing line"—that is, a pipe through which the pump returns the solution directly to the tank instead of to the beds.

When making up a solution, the liquid can then be pumped round and round until the chemicals are dissolved. The valve is then shut off and normal pumping resumed.

If the flume or open channel method is used, then it is easiest to add the chemicals to the channel down which the solution flows from the beds to the sump. The quantity is dumped in the channel, and then spread with a rake as it is carried down into the sump by the flow of solution. This dumping should take place soon after the solution begins to drain away, so that nearly all the solution has to drain through the chemicals before the flow stops. This ensures that none is left undissolved.

In the same way any acid or alkali required is added as the solution flows away. If chemicals are to be added as well, the chemicals should be first, then when the next pumping takes place the pH can be adjusted. To attempt to do the two together would be to court trouble.

Again, when adding make-up water, with a large reservoir hundreds of gallons might be required at one time. If the water is at all alkaline, this would on entering the reservoir in such quantity, precipitate out some of the salts. To avoid this, the water is acidified as it goes into the reservoir. This is done by ascertaining what quantity of acid is needed to bring a small sample down to the required pH. The quantity of water to be added is then calculated from the volume, and the correct amount of acid for that volume poured slowly in at the same time as the water.

This question of dealing in large quantities of water affects the complete changing of the solution. It is often done by halves. For example, every three months or so, or whenever it is decided that a change of solution is desirable, instead of pumping out all the old solution and making up afresh, half is pumped away and made up with plain water. Chemicals to bring this half-volume to the correct composition are also added, not forgetting that the *pH* of the reservoir contents must not fluctuate violently.

Finally, working with a large quantity of nutrient solution, in one way results in simpler operation. This is because there is no need to attempt to work to such narrow limits in the number of parts per million of elements being maintained. What is done is to fix upper and lower limits and to range between them.

Here is a typical example of working limits, quoting from figures used in an American installation:

Element Or Radical	Required Parts Per Million	Limits Upper	Limits Lower
Magnesium	72	96	48
Calcium	360	440	280
Potassium	273	350	195
Nitrate	434	550	310
Phosphate	285	380	190
Sulphate	1,008	1,488	480
Chloride	—	108	—

In practice, the concentration of phosphate, for example, is allowed to drop until tests show that it has reached 190 p.p.m. Enough chemical is then added to bring it up to 380, and then it is again allowed to drop and the process repeated.

Each grower will have to decide for himself his limits according to the solution being used. It is wiser to work to limits that are too narrow rather than too wide, and to keep a close watch on the plants to see that no adverse effects are becoming evident.

11

SOILLESS CULTURE FOR EDUCATION

IF there is one sphere in which there can be no argument as to the value of soilless culture, it is that of teaching plant physiology.

If water culture is used, and transparent jars are the solution containers, root development can be observed in a way with which no other method can compare. The effects of giving too much or too little of the various elements can be tried and noted. The results of too much or too little aeration can be seen. By warming the solution the importance of temperatures can be studied. None of these studies are possible in anything like so convenient a way if soil is used. With water or pure sand culture, the nutrient factor is under complete control and can be varied for whichever purpose is desired.

Seed development, too, can be studied by the germination of seeds in dishes of dilute nutrient solution. In fact, this is one of the tests for the suitability of an aggregate or sand. The method is to take, say, 100 seeds (or 50 would do) and place them on the sand or aggregate in a shallow dish. Dilute solution (about one-quarter strength is ideal) is poured in so that it half-covers the medium. With a pair of tweezers the seeds are then arranged so that they are resting on the particles just touching, but not covered by, the solution. Then cover the dish with a sheet of thick paper and place in a warm spot to germinate.

When the primary root emerges from the seed, if the aggregate is suitable, the root can be observed (through a watchmaker's glass) to grow normally, and produce root hairs in abundance. If the aggregate is toxic, the root may shrivel, or at least curl away from the particles.

For a full test, a small unit should be built and the plantlets grown on for several weeks.

Germination tests for the vitality of seeds can be conducted in the same way, the number which push out primary roots being counted and the percentage calculated.

Tests for the suitability of asphalte or other paint are done by this method, but in this case the particles are coated with the paint. Germination may take longer, as paint is water-repellent, but the effect of poisonous material is evident a day or two afterwards.

A number of schools are already using these methods for the study of plant life, and many more would do so if the effectiveness and simplicity of soilless culture for this purpose were realised. Among schools of which I have personal knowledge are Tipton (Staffordshire) Grammar School, and the schools in Leeds with which Mr. J. H. King, head gardener at Leeds University, is associated.

At Tipton the boys became so enthusiastic that they built a greenhouse especially for soilless culture, and at Leeds it was found that even boys backward in many subjects became skilled and attentive in growing without soil.

In America, at rehabilitation hospitals, it was found that ex-Servicemen disabled in such a way as to be incapable of the hard physical labour of normal soil gardening, were able to operate soilless culture units with ease.

At many nurseries in Britain where the grower is as yet undecided whether to venture on large-scale nutrient culture, a small bed or plot is maintained in solution culture solely for the purpose of the study of plant detriments. Symptoms produced by nutrient manipulation are studied and compared with those which show themselves in soil-grown plants. In Sussex one large nursery was cured of manganese excess in this way. The discovery of the trouble resulted in the saving of hundreds of pounds annually through turning what had been a losing crop into a paying one.

I have myself seen in the nursery of one man who was reckoned to be a "die-hard" compost and soil convert, a fully-equipped laboratory for the study of soilless culture.

WHAT TO DO

If you are minded to study for yourself the effects of deficiencies in the various elements, here is what to do:

Obtain half a dozen new flower pots, eight inches in diameter, and for each fit up a drip culture unit made out of fruit jars as described in the chapter on sand culture. For the purpose of these experiments pure non-calcareous sand must be used. As the amount required is so small, this will not involve a great deal of expense even if the sand has to be bought especially for this purpose.

Fill the pots as already described, not forgetting the test for drainage. Wash the sand with clean rain water or distilled water. Water of this kind must also be used for making up the solutions. In this case, tap or well water will not do, as it may introduce some of the very element which you are trying to do without.

In doing deficiency experiments, the stock solution

method is best. Each salt is made in a separate concentrated solution, and the appropriate mixture made up for dilution as the final growing solution. For the purpose of simplicity we will work in ounces and pints.

The weights in the table below are each dissolved in two pints of water:

Salt	Weight in ounces
Potassium nitrate	4
Sodium nitrate	$3\frac{1}{2}$
Monocalcium phosphate	$2\frac{1}{4}$
Magnesium sulphate	4
Potassium sulphate	4
Sodium sulphate (Glauber salts)	3
Calcium sulphate (plaster of Paris)	3
Sodium acid phosphate	3

The calcium sulphate will not actually dissolve, but will be in what is called "suspension" in the water. Before using, it should therefore be well shaken each time.

Trace elements.

	Weight in ounces
Iron ammonium citrate	1
Manganese sulphate	$\frac{1}{2}$ ⎫ in *one* pint
Boric Acid	$\frac{1}{2}$ ⎭

The iron citrate should be dissolved in hot water. Add two fluid ounces of the manganese and boron solution to the citrate solution. Label this "Trace elements".

The various solutions are then prepared as follows:

NORMAL SOLUTION

Salt	*Amount of Stock Solution in fluid ounces*
Potassium nitrate	4
Sodium nitrate	4
Monocalcium phosphate	2
Magnesium sulphate	4
Trace elements	$\frac{1}{2}$

Make up the solution by pouring three pints of water into a container, add each amount of stock solution separately, stirring each time, and then make up to a final volume of half a gallon. This is the complete stock solution. For use, it must be diluted with nine parts of rain or distilled water.

MINUS NITROGEN

Salt	*Amount in fluid ounces*
Potassium sulphate	$4\frac{1}{2}$
Sodium sulphate	3

Remainder as with normal solution.

MINUS PHOSPHOROUS

Salt	*Amount in fluid ounces*
Calcium sulphate	2

This is used instead of the monocalcium phosphate. Remainder as with normal solution.

TISSUE TESTS

Another interesting field for experiment and study is that of tissue tests. Although I do not consider the full range of solution analyses either necessary or desirable in most cases, tissue tests should not be overlooked. They are qualitative, rather than quantitative. The same degree of accuracy is not really required, and the lessons learned are of value rather from comparison with other plants and with past experience than from actual values noted.

They can, therefore, be done with more confidence by those whose experience of plants is greater than their experience of chemistry.

Although tissue tests are of chief interest when something has gone wrong and it is desired to find out *what*, they must also be carried out on normally-growing plants so that the grower can learn what to expect when things are going well, and so know the difference when things are not.

If you wanted, you could find out how much of all the major and minor elements are present in the plant by cutting up the tissues, extracting with acid, and analysing the extract. But tests for nitrogen and phosphorous are all that are really of interest to the practical man.

Let us take the phosphorous test first, since if you have already decided to go in for the phosphate test of aggregate you will have the apparatus and reagents to hand. They are exactly the same as for the aggregate test, but instead of testing the extract from the gravel you test the extract from the plant. This is taken in the following way:

MINUS POTASSIUM

Omit potassium nitrate, but use double the amount of sodium nitrate. Remainder as with normal solution.

MINUS CALCIUM

Salt	Amount in fluid ounces
Sodium acid phosphate	2

This is used instead of monocalcium phosphate. Remainder as with normal solution.

MINUS MAGNESIUM

Omit magnesium sulphate and use double the amount of sodium sulphate (i.e. 8 fluid ounces).

MINUS IRON AND TRACE ELEMENTS

Simply omit this solution from the final concentrate.

One of the best crops to grow for such experiments is the tomato. It is so sensitive to nutrient changes that it is known as—and used as—an "indicator" plant. In former times they were even used in mines to indicate the presence of coal gas which could not be detected by the human nose.

Sow the tomatoes in sand in a seed-box, but water them with rain or distilled water only. When the seed leaves appear give half-strength *normal* solution, and when ready, pot into thumb pots, still using the half-strength normal solution. A week or so before planting out into the eight-inch pots give full-strength normal solution.

One of the most practical ways of doing this is to obtain one of those large developing trays that photographers use, and stand the pots in it. When you feed, all you have to do is to pour the solution into the tray and the pots will suck up what they need. Be sure, however, that the tray is level, otherwise some of the plants may not get any solution. It is important that the feeding should be equal, because the plants at the start of the experiment should be as uniform as possible.

When three inches or so tall, plant out into the eight-inch pots, and begin feeding through the inverted jars. From this stage on, each jar will contain its own solution, and the experiment will be on.

The effects of the deficiencies will not be fully evident for several weeks. When they do, the following will be noted:

MINUS NITROGEN

Foliage light green, yellowing, then dying. Leaves small and stems thin. The plant takes on a distinctive "erect" posture, with the branches pointing upwards instead of outwards. If you are imaginative, you can think of it as holding up supplicating hands for more food.

MINUS PHOSPHOROUS

There is no mistaking this. The leaves turn dark bluish green, changing to a purplish tinge, especially underneath. They have a distinct downward curl, and unlike leaves that die from nitrogen deficiency, they drop off quickly.

MINUS POTASSIUM

The lower leaves show dead pale grey areas near the ti[ps] and margins, which is called "potassium scorch". On[e] of the characteristics is that the leaves die from the marg[in] inwards. Dark pin-point spots on the lower leaves a[nd] stems spread until the plant dies.

MINUS CALCIUM

Unlike the symptoms already described, those of [cal]cium shortage show themselves on the young leaves [at] growing tip first. The leaflets take on a pronoun[ced] hook at the tip. Then they go yellow and purple and [die] off.

MINUS MAGNESIUM

One of the swiftest effects to appear. The distin[ct] thing to watch for is that while the veins of the l[ower] leaves stay green, the blade between goes yellow and [red]. If this occurs at the top of the plant, it indicates [iron] deficiency, but at the bottom it points to magnesium [. A] further distinction is that whereas the magnesium [effect] is seen all over the leaf, with iron it is centred ne[ar the] base.

By growing one plant alongside the others, bu[t in] normal solution, valuable comparisons can be made[.] There is no better way of learning and remember[ing] symptoms for which to watch.

Although the effects noted are on the tomato, m[ost of] them also apply to a number of other crops, for wh[ich they] are a useful guide.

Take a few sections of leaf petiole (the stem between the base of the leaf and the main branch) and chop up into fine discs with a razor blade. Weight about 2·5 grams and put into a glass beaker. Add 25 ml. of Morgan's extractant (previously described). Allow to stand for fifteen minutes, stirring occasionally with a clean glass rod. Filter, and the resultant liquid is tested as for the previous test. In this case, however, the results should be multiplied by ten to correct for the extraction ratio.

The nitrate test is very simple. The reagent used is diphenylamine, which is very corrosive, and should be kept away from the hands and clothing. It is also very sensitive, and everything used in connection with it must be scrupulously clean.

One other feature of this reagent is that it deteriorates rapidly under conditions of high temperature or in sunlight. It must be tested periodically, and discarded as soon as it gives a positive test with distilled water.

The reagent is made by dissolving one gram of diphenylamine in 100 ml. concentrated sulphuric acid.

The simplest way of applying the test is to make a small diagonal cut across the petiole of a leaf and add one drop to the cut surface.

This must be done at the same time of the day, and to the same part of the plant, with each different test, otherwise comparisons lose their value.

Normal nitrogen condition gives a dark blue to blue black colour. Low nitrate gives a green to pale blue colour. No nitrate shows as a brown to brownish black colour. Sometimes it is difficult to tell whether the colour is blue black or brown black. In this case make another cut and add a drop of concentrated sulphuric acid. If the black colour develops, this is simply the action of the acid and not a true indication of nitrate.

Another very useful practice, particularly with the

minor elements, is that of checking for deficiencies by means of dilute solutions of the element suspected to be deficient. The method of doing this is as follows:

Choose a half-grown leaf, if anything nearer the top of the plant than the bottom. With a pair of sharp scissors, cut off the tip of the leaf about one-eighth of the way along the mid-rib. Arrange a small jar of the test solution (a fish-paste jar is about the right size and shape) tied in such a position that the cut tip dips into it. If necessary the stem on which the leaf is situated can be weighed down with a small weight to cause the leaf to remain in the solution. The tip should be left in for ten hours, and the jar then removed. If the deficient element is the one supplied in the solution, the leaf will show a response in seven to ten days.

Among dilutions which have been recommended for this test are:

>   Iron   0·25% solution of ferrous sulphate.
>   Copper   0·3% solution of copper sulphate.
>   Magnesium and
>   potassium   0·5% solution of the sulphate.

EXAMPLE: 0·5 gr. of magnesium sulphate in 100 c.c. water.

The iron and magnesium tests are especially striking, often changing the whole colour and texture of a leaf which is deficient in one or other of these elements. The same method, however, may be tried with almost any element vital to growth.

For school work, where it is simply intended to show how a plant grows, it is probably best to use the water culture method. Quart fruit jars with corks in the mouths are the most suitable containers, and should be wrapped round with dark brown paper held in place with an elastic band. When giving lessons, the teacher can then either remove the band to show the roots, or even lift out the entire plant. If it is replaced carefully and not kept out too long, no harm results.

By growing several such plants side by side, the effects of proper aeration can be seen. One plant can be aerated, say, for fifteen minutes daily by bubbling through the solution. Another can be aerated for five minutes, and another not at all. It is surprising how great a difference to growth even such a small difference in culture can make.

For this purpose almost any kind of suitable plant can be used. Perhaps bulbs are the best, and later on in the season, coleus.

Similarly, plants can be grown in solutions adjusted to the various *pH* values, and the differences noted. This is one of the most telling ways of bringing home to would-be gardeners the importance of lime to proper growth.

12

WHERE HAVE I GONE WRONG?

"Have a heart," I can hear you saying; "you have been giving us warnings on nearly every page, and now you propose to devote a whole chapter to them!"

The comment is a sound one. It is true that at the risk of seeming to be discouraging I have pointed out the pitfalls rather than avoided them. It is also true that if you start soilless culture—or anything else for that matter—with all the negatives in mind and few of the positives, you will be stepping off on the wrong foot.

Yet there are so many who have blithely mixed a curious concoction and left their plants to its doubtful mercies, that I really must insist on this collection of "don'ts". If you like, you can look on the bright side, and use it only for reference if anything goes wrong. But I think you would be wiser to read on.

Before we deal with the subject in detail, one general piece of advice must be underlined. Soilless culture is not a system in which anything can be left to chance. When you are growing in soil, you can assume that if you put a seed into a portion of soil—any soil, anywhere—it will grow. You will be wrong, often, but you will be right often enough to justify the assumption. Nature sees to that. In soilless culture, however, in a way YOU are Nature. YOU are providing the substitute for soil. And just as Nature takes care of everything, you must be prepared, in this instance, to do the same.

So neglect no detail. Do not imagine, that as you have

WHERE HAVE I GONE WRONG?

got most things right, the others will follow. They may not. So in this, as in so many things, prevention is better than cure.

We may consider possible difficulties under three main headings:

1. The solution;
2. The apparatus, including the tanks, beds, pumps and pipes; and
3. The management.

THE SOLUTION

Theoretical. Simple as it may seem, one of the mistakes often made is that of faulty arithmetic in working out the amounts of salts required. See that you have measured the volume of your solution container correctly. Check your decimal points. Go over your conversion figures from grams to ounces and litres to gallons, if you are converting.

Remember, if you are using a solution given in an American publication in gallons, that these are different from Imperial gallons. One U.S. gallon equals 0·833 of one of ours.

Go over your salts, and make sure that they *are* what you think they are. Monocalcium phosphate can be in a number of different forms, each with a different amount of phosphorous. Magnesium sulphate can be anhydrous or the more usual kind, the hydrated Epsom Salts. Calcium sulphate can be gypsum or Plaster of Paris. Each has a different calcium content.

Be sure you are not using too great a proportion of ammonium nitrogen.

Practical. Are you sure you have weighed the salts

correctly? You have not, for example, worked out a formula in grams and then weighed it in ounces? The question may seem fatuous, but I have known it done.

Are your scales working correctly, or is there perhaps a weight hiding underneath the pan, and preventing it going down, without being seen?

Are you dissolving the salts in the correct order? Have you made sure of the composition of the water, or have you left it to chance?

Have you been spraying your plants or greenhouse with some anti-insect or anti-disease preparation, and allowed some to get into the solution? This practice may often cause plant injury.

Is your water supply, although chemically correct, perhaps being subjected to special treatment owing to exceptional conditions, such as chlorine treatment during an epidemic?

If you are relying on the chemical testing and replacement method, are you sure of your reagents, or may one or more of them have deteriorated, and been giving a false reading? Have you tested them against a standard solution to check this?

Are you checking the *pH* often enough? Are you carrying out the *pH* test in the correct way? If the test is taken before the acid or alkali, which may have been used for adjustment, is properly dispersed in the solution, the reading may be wrong. Are the test-tubes used for the test clean, or have they been laying about the greenhouse for days getting dirty and perhaps chemically coated?

Did you wash out the tank on replacing the solution, or did chemical residues from the previous mix remain at the bottom?

Are you maintaining the water level regularly, especially in hot weather?

Is your solution much below the temperature of the air where the plants are growing?

What about the vessels in which you mix your stock solutions, if you use them? Are they beyond suspicion, or have you thought it of no importance?

THE APPARATUS

Beds. Trouble from this source might be due to:

1. Faulty construction, resulting in incomplete drainage and pools around the roots. One example of this is building a ground bed on heavy clay soil without making arrangements for surplus water to get away.
2. Unsuitable materials, such as uncoated galvanised iron, or even drainage tiles containing elements like manganese.
3. Detrimental contacts, such as iron touching copper in contact with the solution, resulting in the iron going into solution.
4. Clogging of drainage.
5. Unsuitable media, either too coarse, or too fine.
6. Poisonous media, such as fresh cinders, containing boron.
7. Accumulations of salts through using too strong a solution, or not leaching the aggregate.
8. Diseases or even insects in the media. The remedy for this is sterilisation.
9. Calcareous media, for which allowance has not been made in calculating the solution.
10. Black paint which *looks* like non-toxic asphalte paint, but in fact is not.

Tanks. Among the mistakes are:

1. Using galvanised tanks without asphalting them.
2. Not having them low enough below the bed to allow for prompt and complete drainage.
3. Too small a volume.
4. Below the water level, so that in wet weather water drains over into them and upsets the balance of the solution.
5. Unsuspected leaks that cause frequent replenishment of water thought to be taken up by the plants, but which has actually drained away.
6. Placing in a position exposed to strong light, which causes precipitation of iron.

Pumps and pipes. Faults here might be:

1. Unsuitable materials, resulting in corrosion and pollution of the solution.
2. Choked pumps, causing very slow flow.
3. Pipes of too small a bore, again causing a slow flow.
4. Too slow pumping and drainage, leading to insufficient aeration.
5. In the drip method, blockage through the growth of algae at the feed holes.
6. Insufficient power to force solution evenly to all areas of large installation.

Management of the solution. Points to watch in this respect are:

1. The right frequency of pumping. Not too often and not too seldom.

2. In sand culture, applying only when the feel of the sand indicates that solution is needed.

3. Avoidance of wetting foliage of plants susceptible to damage from this cause.

4. Regular and complete replacement, or regular and accurate testing to make up nutrients used up.

5. Proper level of pumping, high for seedlings and young plants, and lower for larger ones.

6. Proper aeration if the water culture method is being used.

7. Do not allow solution used for hand-fed units to stand about in galvanised cans or buckets.

8. Avoid dripping concentrated solution on leaves, particularly young ones. This often causes burning.

In addition to the detriments possible under the above headings, certain other conditions may lead to trouble. Many industrial gases, particularly coal gas used in kitchen stoves, are very poisonous to plants. House conservatories of the lean-to type with a door leading to a kitchen or out-house where gas is used are frequently offenders in this respect. Oil burners can have the same effect.

Many of the fumigants, if improperly used or if the fumes are not properly cleared away, can lead to growth problems. Soilless culture media is usually much more easily permeable than soil, and where no harm would result in the normal way, it cannot be ruled out with aggregate unless extra care is used.

In most cases such trouble can be ameliorated or removed by thorough flushing with plain water.

DISEASES

Although the incidence of them is much reduced, all the above-ground pests and diseases may occur without soil just as with it. Bacterial, fungoid, and virus diseases call for the same treatment as with soil, bearing in mind the greater care needed to allow as little as possible of the spray or powder used to penetrate the aggregate.

In some cases it is advisable to flood the bed with plain water during the spraying or dusting, and then drain it away before pumping in normal solution again.

Keeping the top surface of the sand or gravel dry is a good insurance against troubles of the mildew type which attack the lower leaves or stems.

Seed-borne plant diseases such as damping off can be obviated by the use of seed-treating chemicals, many of which are on the market. In soilless culture, however, it is advisable to use them at as low a strength as possible to avoid contamination of the solution. One of the most practical methods of treating seeds is to make up a one per cent. solution of formalin. Cover the seeds with twice the volume occupied by the seeds (such as two pints of solution to one of seed) and soak for fifteen minutes, stirring every five minutes. Afterwards the seeds should be spread out and dried either in the air or in very gentle heat.

There is a certain amount of evidence that at least one of the well-known root diseases may be transferred from bed to bed of multiple units by the solution. It is important therefore to see that drainings from soil do not get into the beds or solutions, and that soil, the purity of which is suspected, is not allowed to get into the aggregate.

INSECTS

Birds, ants, and other insects can cause trouble in soilless gardens, and in fact in some cases more trouble than in soil because of the easier access to seeds between the larger media particles. The same remedies of dusting, spraying and netting can be used.

Snails and crawling insects, however, appear to be discouraged by rough or sharp particles. Fortunately, on the other hand, the quick-moving insects, which are usually harmless to plants since they prey on the slower insects, appear to find sand and gravel beds quite congenial.

OTHER FACTORS

With soilless culture units out of doors, special attention has to be paid to the possibility of wind damage. The plants are not anchored so strongly as in soil, and a comparatively light wind may do a good deal of damage. It is important to site such beds in the shelter of natural windbreaks, or if none such are available, to construct some of temporary fencing.

With outdoor installations, too, rain, instead of being beneficial, can be harmful, if it is so heavy as to leach away the chemicals from the media, or to dilute the solution in the tank so much as to unbalance it. The remedy, with sand beds, is to re-apply solution after a heavy and prolonged period of rain, and with sub-irrigation beds to cover the tank to keep out the rain and divert the drainage down a separate outlet away from the tanks.

In some cases, owing to the dry nature of the top of the gravel or sand, hot sunshine in midsummer may cause such arid conditions that it is beneficial to cover the top of the aggregate. Glass wool, thin strips of asbestos, sacking, and even fern leaves and the like have been used. In general, the trouble involved in such practices is not warranted by actual results, and the normal English summer seldom produces long enough spells of intensive sunshine to call for their use.

Removal of old plants from sand or gravel requires rather a different technique from soil. The best method is to cut off all but the top few inches of plant, and then, grasping the stump firmly, to pull out steadily and smoothly so as to remove as much as possible of the roots. With sand this is usually easier than with coarser media, in which some roots have a tendency to cling. After a number of successive crops, roots may be found to accumulate in the media. This should be combed through with a fine rake to remove as many as possible. If the accumulation at the bottom of the bed is heavy enough to slow up filling and draining, it may be necessary to take out all the media, clean the bottom, and replace.

TASTE AND FOOD VALUE

Some growers have occasionally encountered what may be termed a difficulty in that customers say they can distinguish a "chemical" taste with soilless grown products. Usually this is pure imagination. Extensive tests have been carried out on soilless grown tomatoes, lettuce, radish, cucumber and several other food crops.

The results have shown that there is no significant difference in taste between properly grown soil or soilless crops. The quality is as good, the keeping qualities as good or better, and the nutritional value as great. The mineral and vitamin content is essentially the same.

It is a fact, however, that soil-grown crops contain comparatively larger amounts of extraneous minerals, such as aluminium, silicon, and fluorine. These are apparently absorbed by the plants along with essential elements. They are of no value to human beings, however, and do not affect the food value in any way.

PROPAGATION

Contrary to some published statements, there is no evidence at all that seed or cuttings from soilless cultivated plants are any less vigorous than from soil-grown ones. Ten or more generations of good-cropping tomatoes have been successively grown from plants out of soil for all that time. Many carnation nurseries have propagated only from sand-cultivated plants for ten years or more.

13

THE FUTURE

AMONG thinking gardeners and growers there appear to be two principal views on the future of soilless culture. They are:

1. That it is a mere flash-in-the-pan; a novelty that will die out before many years have passed; and,
2. That it is the coming thing, and will eventually be the accepted practice in all greenhouse work, as well as in conditions where soil growth is not possible.

The protagonists for the first, point to the undoubted number of people who have taken up chemical solution culture and later abandoned it; to the also undoubted facts of its higher costs and skill requirements; and to the fact that good soil well cultivated can provide anything we are likely to require.

No one in their senses would deny that soil is the ideal medium for growth. In good heart, it provides all the food plants need. It retains moisture. It provides good root support. It is well-nigh universal.

All these statements are undeniable. Yet despite them, soilless culture has a definite place in the horticultural scene. The claim to this place is established on the following grounds:

(a) In some parts of the world the soil is so poor or disease-ridden that it is impossible to grow crops in the normal way.

(b) In intense under-glass culture, conditions have already become so artificial that there is no logical reason for denying the use of artificial growth media.

(c) It is the best way of learning the effects of excesses or deficiencies of fertilisers.

(d) It is a useful and fascinating hobby.

To prove the first of these arguments, one has only to point to the achievements of the U.S. Army Air Force at tropical centres during the last war. Without soilless culture large numbers of their forces stationed in inaccessible outposts would have been without fresh vegetables.

Early in 1945 the first installation was established on Ascension Island, a particularly difficult place on which to start. It was an ideal place to prove the value of the system, since the only soil was a small pocket near the top of the volcanic rock of which the island is largely comprised. Close on 100,000 lb. of vegetables (chiefly tomatoes, lettuces and cucumbers) were produced during the first year.

A few months later a second installation was built in British Guiana, take-off point for the transatlantic aircraft. This contained 75 beds—three times the number on Ascension. This time the yield in the first year of operation (1946) was nearly 240,000 lb.

A third installation was begun, again in 1945, at Iwo Jima; and the decision was also made to begin the world's biggest installation in Japan.

This venture, on two separate hydroponic farms, comprised a total of 80 acres. The undertaking was so large that it warrants description in some detail. The farms were made of units of five acres, each containing 87 beds covering an area 300 feet by four feet. One unit at Chofu, Tokyo, was under glass; the others were in the open.

In British territory, the Bahamas provide an example of a part of the world where soilless culture can be of great benefit. In some areas of these islands the soil is so poor and thin that only one crop of tomatoes can be produced. The "farm" then has to move on to fresh ground. With soilless culture, on the other hand, the same site can be used indefinitely.

The development of soilless culture for general greenhouse work is the biggest question mark. Even the most optimistic enthusiast would hesitate to predict large scale development in this field until the cost of installation is lower than it is today. Capital expenditure for soil work is so high that to add the extra cost of aggregate tanks and beds, with all their ancillary equipment, too often makes the project prohibitive. But in my view there is no doubt that as labour difficulties increase, and as the younger generation of growers, more versed in chemical knowledge, takes the helm, the number of nurseries operated on soilless lines will increase.

Already the virtual disappearance of the horse population of the British Isles has forced many growers to use artificial instead of natural manures, and it is not difficult to envisage a time when there will be a fairly general turning over from chemically-improved soil to chemically-nourished aggregate.

One of the features of the development of soilless culture that is often overlooked is that the subject is still in its infancy. Not all the techniques have been explored, even in a perfunctory manner. Already the preliminary research has been conducted into a method which would have some of the "fool-proof" aspects of growth in good soil. Instead of applying the nutrients by means of a

THE FUTURE

solution, an entirely different principle is possible. This is the principle of "ion exchange".

The subject is a difficult one for the lay-man, but perhaps it is simplest to explain that when a chemical salt dissolves in water, it is split up into positive and negative charges known as "ions". This phenomenon is used to cause ions to become "adsorbed" on a synthetic material, one form of which is Amberlite resin. This material is saturated, as it were, with nutrient—as are the clay particles in ordinary soil—which, when water is applied gradually becomes available to plants rooted in it. The "charged" ion-exchange material is mixed with sand, and the mixture placed in beds in the ordinary way. All that then has to be done is to supply water.

All the mixing and testing is provided for in the initial "charging", so that the material becomes in effect a complete artificial soil.

Although very promising results were achieved experimentally with this technique, it has not yet reached the commercial, or even the small-scale practical, stage. There is no doubt, however, that sooner or later work on these lines will again come into prominence.

Much depends on the food situation of the world. If some of the international food experts' predictions come true, it may well be that in the years to come, the world will need every method of food production of which it is capable, and that soilless culture will then be called upon to supply a vital need.

APPENDIX

METRIC TABLES

Table of Length

(Km)	1 Kilometre	equals	1,000	metres
(Hm)	1 Hektometre	,,	100	metres
(Dm)	1 Dekametre	,,	10	metres
(m)	1 Metre	,,	100	cm. or 1,000 mm.
(dm)	1 decimetre	,,	0·1	metre
(cm)	1 centimetre	,,	0·01	metre
(mm)	1 millimetre	,,	0·001	metre

Table of Weight

(Kg)	1 Kilogram	equals	1,000	grams
(Hg)	1 Hektogram	,,	100	grams
(Dg)	1 Dekagram	,,	10	grams
(g)	1 gram	,,	weight	of 1 c.c. water or 1,000 mg.
(dg)	1 decigram	,,	0·1	gram
(cg)	1 centigram	,,	0·01	gram
(mg)	1 milligram	,,	0·001	gram

Table of Capacity

(Kl)	1 Kilolitre	equals	1,000	litres
(Hl)	1 Hektolitre	,,	100	litres
(Dl)	1 Dekalitre	,,	10	litres
(l)	1 litre	,,	1,000	cub. centimetres
(dl)	1 decilitre	,,	0·1	litre (100 c.c.)
(cl)	1 centilitre	,,	0·01	litre (10 c.c.)
(ml)	1 millilitre	,,	0·001	litre (1 c.c.)

It will be readily seen from the above table that 1 milligram of substance dissolved in 1 litre of water gives 1 part per million (1 p.p.m.) of that substance in water (or 1 gram in 1,000 litres).

CONVERSION TABLES

1. *Linear Measure*

Imperial			Metric	
1 inch	25·4	mm.	1 mm.	0·039 in.
1 foot	0·305	m.	1 cm. (10 mm.)	0·394 in.
1 yard	0·9144 m.		1 dm. (10 cm.)	3·937 in.
1 mile	1·609	km.	1 m.	{ 39·370 in. / 3·281 ft. / 1·093 yds.
			1 km	0·621 mile

2. *Square Measure*

Imperial		Metric	
1 sq. in.	6·451 sq. cm.	1 sq. cm.	0·155 sq. in.
1 sq. yd.	0·836 sq. m.	1 sq. m.	10·764 sq. ft.
			1·196 sq. yds.

3. *Cubic Measure*

Imperial		Metric	
1 cub. in.	16·387 cub. cm.	1 cub. cm.	0·061 cub. in.
		1 cub. cm.	61·024 cub. in.
1 cub. ft.	0·038 cub. m.	1 cub. m.	35·315 cub. ft.
1 cub. yd.	0·764 cub. m.		1·308 cub. yds.

4. *Measure of Weight*

Imperial		Metric	
1 oz.	28·3 grams.		
1 lb.	0·454 kg.	1 kg.	2·204 lb.
1 ton	1,016 kg.		

5. *Measures of Capacity*

Imperial		Metric	
1 pint	0.568 l.	1 l.	1·759 pints
1 gallon	4·546 l.		·22 gal.
		1 hl.	175·98 pints
			21·997 gals.

APPENDIX

To convert yards to metres, multiply by 0·914.
To convert gallons to litres, multiply by 4·54.
To convert litres to gallons, multiply by 0·22.

ATOMIC WEIGHTS

The following table of atomic weights refers only to those elements most generally used in soilless culture.

Element	Symbol	Atomic weight Exact	Approximate
Aluminium	Al	26·97	27
Boron	B	10·82	11
Calcium	Ca	40·08	40
Carbon	C	12·01	12
Chlorine	Cl	35·457	35
Copper	Cu	63·57	64
Hydrogen	H	1·0078	1
Iron	Fe	55·84	56
Magnesium	Mg	24·32	24
Manganese	Mn	54·93	55
Nitrogen	N	14·008	14
Oxygen	O	16·0	16
Phosphorus	P	31·02	31
Potassium	K	39·096	39
Silicon	Si	28·06	28
Sodium	Na	22·997	23
Sulphur	S	32·06	32
Zinc	Zn	65.38	65

CONVERSION FACTORS

1 inch	=	2·54 c.m.
1 c.m.	=	0·394 inch
1 pound	=	453·6 grams

To convert yards to metres, multiply by 0·914

To convert lb. avoirdupois to kilograms, multiply by 0·454

To convert gallons to litres, multiply by 4·54

To convert ounces to grams, multiply by 28·3

MISCELLANEOUS USEFUL FACTORS

1 litre = 0·88 quart or 1·76 pints.

Ounces per gallon multiplied by 6·25 = grams per litre.

Grams per litre multiplied by 1·6 = ounces per 10 gallons.

One U.S. gallon = 0·833 Imperial gallon.

1 Quart weighs roughly 4 oz. avoirdupois.

1° Centigrade = 1·8° Fahrenheit.

1 Cubic foot = $6\frac{1}{4}$ gallons.

To convert weight of 50% calcium nitrate solution into measure of capacity, multiply by $4/3$.

TWO SUGGESTED FORMULÆ FOR BEGINNERS*

Salt	Amount in ounces	In level teaspoonful
Potassium phosphate	½	1
Potassium nitrate	2	4
Calcium nitrate	3	7
Epsom salts	1½	4
Water	20 gallons	
Ammonium phosphate	½	2
Potassium nitrate	2½	5
Calcium nitrate	2½	6
Epsom salts	1½	4
Water	20 gallons	

To each of these solutions, the usual trace elements have to be added.

*Originated by California Agricultural Experiment Station.

†THE W.P. FORMULA

	Grams per 1,000 litres
Potassium nitrate	608
Gypsum	1,214
Epsom salts	511
Monocalcium phosphate (food grade)	282
Ammonium sulphate	110
	2,725 grams

†Developed by A. Wagner & G. Poesch, Ohio Agricultural Experiment Station.

FORMULÆ WHICH CAN BE MIXED DRY

Simplified Formula for Amateur use:

Potassium nitrate	1 oz.
Monocalcium phosphate	½ oz.
Magnesium sulphate	¾ oz.
Ferrous sulphate	1 teaspoonful
Rain water	4¼ gallons

Commercial Use*

	Grams per 1,000 litres
Potassium nitrate	1,100
Gypsum	760
Epsom salts	520
Monocalcium phosphate (treble super)	310
Ammonium sulphate	140
Total weight as complete mix	2,830 grams

For Calcareous aggregates*

	Grams per 1,000 litres
Potassium nitrate	1,100
Magnesium sulphate†	520
Ammonium phosphate (fertiliser grade)	280

*From *Nutriculture*, the U.S. War Department manual.

†This may require to be reduced or left out if any appreciable quantity of magnesium is found in the aggregate.

GUIDE TO PREPARATION OF NUTRIENT SOLUTIONS*

Chemical	Fraction of one ounce required per 100 gallons to give 1 p.p.m. of element specified.
Sodium nitrate	0·103 N
Calcium nitrate	0·135 N also 1·4 p.p.m. Ca
Ammonium sulphate	0·076 N
Potassium nitrate (for N)	0·122 N also 2·8 p.p.m. K
Potassium nitrate (for K)	0·044 K also 0·36 p.p.m. N
Potassium sulphate	0·040 K
Potassium chloride (muriate)	0·033 K
Superphosphate (16% sol P_2O_5)	0·268 P also 3·8 p.p.m. Ca
Monocalcium phosphate	0·076 P also 0·6 p.p.m. Ca
Monopotassium phosphate	0·07 P 0·056 K
Magnesium sulphate (Epsom salts)	0·172 Mg
Ferrous sulphate	0·089 Fe
Calcium sulphate (gypsum)	0·076 Ca
Calcium sulphate (plaster of Paris)	0·027 Ca
Manganese sulphate	0·065 Mn
Boric acid	0·090 B
Ferric ammonium citrate	0·138 Fe
Diammonium phosphate	0·095 P
Magnesium nitrate	0·13 Mg.

*Based on a table issued by Prof. R. H. Stoughton, D.Sc., of Reading University.

MOLECULAR WEIGHTS
Including usual percentage of impurities

Salt	Formula	Molecular Weight
Ammonium sulphate	$(NH_4)_2SO_4$	140
Sodium nitrate	$NaNO_3$	90
Potassium nitrate	KNO_3	110
Calcium nitrate	$Ca(NO_3)_2.H_2O$	260
Calcium nitrate (pure form)	$Ca(NO_3)_2.$	180
Potassium sulphate	K_2SO_4	200
Potassium chloride	KCL	80
Monocalcium phosphate (super)	—	750
Monocalcium phosphate (treble super)	$CaH_4(PO_4)_2.H_2O$	310
Monocalcium phosphate (food grade)	$CaH_4(PO_4)_2.H_2O$	270
Monopotassium phosphate	KH_2PO_4	140
Magnesium sulphate (Epsom salts)	$MgSO_4.7H_2O$	260
Magnesium sulphate anhydrous	$MgSO_4$	130
Calcium sulphate (plaster of Paris)	$CaSO_4$	190
Calcium chloride	$Ca\ Cl_2$	150
Ammonium phosphate	$NH_4H_2PO_4$	140
Ammonium phosphate (food grade)	$NH_4H_2PO_4$	120
Magnesium nitrate	$Mg(NO_3)_2.6H_2O$	256

RELATIONS OF ANTAGONISM

(The elements, an excess of which will inhibit the uptake of other elements).

Except in the case of those underlined, the first element inhibits the uptake of the second. In the underlined cases it assists the uptake.

N/K	N/P	<u>N/Mg</u>			
K/Mg	<u>K/Fe</u>	K/Mn	K/Ca	K/Mg	K/N
Mg/Ca	Mg/K	Mg/N			
Na/Ca					
Ca/Mn	Ca/B	Ca/N	Ca/K	Ca/Mg	
P/Zn					
Mn/Fe	Heavy metals/*Fe*				
Fe/Mn					

BIBLIOGRAPHY

WITHROW, R. B. and BIEBEL, J. P. *Nutrient Solution Methods of Greenhouse Crop Production*, Purdue University, October, 1938.

SHIVE, J. W. and ROBBINS, W. R. *Methods of Growing Plants in Solution and Sand Cultures*, (New Jersey Agricultural Experiment Station Bulletin, September, 1938).

TURNER, W. and HENRY, V. M. *Growing Plants in Nutrient Solutions*. Chapman & Hall Ltd. (1939, reprinted 1948).

PHILLIPS, A. H. *Gardening Without Soil*. C. Arthur Pearson Ltd., (1940).

LAURIE, ALEX. *Soilless Culture Simplified*. McGraw-Hill Book Co., Inc., New York, (1940).

GERICKE, DR. W. F. *Soilless Gardening*. Prentice-Hall, Inc., U.S.A. (1940).

HILYER, C. ISABEL. *Hydroponics*. Penguin Books, London, (1940).

STOUGHTON, DR. R. H. *Soilless Cultivation of Plants*. Journal R. H. S. Vol. 61. Part I, (1941).

KIPLINGER, D. C. and LAURIE, ALEX. *Growing Ornamental Greenhouse Crops in Gravel Culture*. Ohio Agricultural Experiment Station, (October, 1942).

STOUGHTON, DR. R. H. *Review of Recent Progress*, Journal Ministry of Agriculture, (1942, 49).

PHILLIPS, A. H. *The Science of Soilless Culture*. C. Arthur Pearson Ltd., (1943).

NICHOLAS, D. J. D. *The Diagnosis of Mineral Deficiencies in Crops by Means of Chemical Tissue Tests*. The Tintometer Ltd., Salisbury, (1944).

FAWCETT, G. S. and STOUGHTON, DR. R. H. *The Chemical Testing of Plant Nutrient Solutions*. The Tintometer Ltd., (1944).

BIBLIOGRAPHY

EDWARDS, K. B. *Heated Sand Culture for the Week-end Gardener*, Journal R. H. S., 71 (2), (1946).

STILES, PROF., W. *Trace Elements in Plants.* (Cambridge University Press, 1946).

U.S. ARMY PUBLICATIONS DEPT. *Nutriculture,* (1946).

TEMPLEMAN, DR. W. G. *The Culture of Plants in Sand and in Aggregate.* Imperial Chemical Industries, (March 1947).

ELLIS C., SWANEY, M. W. and EASTWOOD, T. *Soilless Growth of Plants.* Reinhold Publishing Corpn., New York, (1947).

STOUGHTON, DR. R. H. *Nutrient Solution Culture, Journal* Ministry of Agriculture, 1947 (53).

PURDUE UNIVERSITY. *Nutriculture,* (1948).

MUSSENBROCK, A, and BEACH, G. *Cost Comparison—Soil and Gravel Carnations.* (Proc. American Society Hort., Science, June, 1948).

CARNATION SOCIETY. *Soilless Cultivation of Perpetual Carnations.* British Carnation Society, London, (1949).

NICHOLAS, D. J. *Chemical Tissue Tests for Plants.* Bristol University, (April 1949).

TICQUET, C. E. *Some Common Mistakes.* The Fruitgrower, No. 2789, June 1949.

SIMPSON, A. J. *Flowers and Vegetables without Soil.* The London Gardens Society, October, 1949.

HOAGLAND, D. R. and ARNON, D. I. *The Water Culture Method of Growing Plants Without Soil.* (University of California, 1950).

TICQUET, C. E. *The Future of Soilless Culture.* (Journal Ministry of Agriculture, 56, 11 February, 1950).

INDEX

Acid additions, 46
Adsorption, 55
Aeration, 61
Aggregates, 112
Algae, 114
Alkali additions, 45
Ammonium salts, 25, 30, 34, 46
Analysis of solutions, 49
Analysis of media, 110
Annual flowers, 70
Asbestos, 57, 89, 117
Ascension, 161
Asphalte, 58
Asphalte mastic, 117
Atmospheres, 48
Atomic weights, 22, 167
Automatic feeding, 81

Bahamas, 162
Balance, Chemical, 37
Beans, 69
Beetroot, 97
Begonias, 71
Boron, 34
Boussingault, J., 9
Brick beds, 102
British Guiana, 161
Bucket units, 99
Bulbs, 70
Buffer action, 46

Cabbage, 67
Calcareous media, 75, 112
Calcium salts, 33
Carnations, 53, 87, 96, 125
Carrots, 67
Cascade system, 62
Chlorine, 15
Cinders, 109, 112
Cinders test, 78
Clinker, 109
Coleus, 83
Commercial units, 114
Comparators, 44
Concentrations, 48
Concrete beds, 117
Conversion tables, 116
Copper gauze, 80, 103
Copper sulphate, 34
Corms, 70
Cucumbers, 65
Cuttings, 96

Daffodil, 71
Dahlias, 71
Damping off, 156
De Saussure, 9
Deficiency experiments, 140
Deficiency symptoms, 144
Direct feed units, 102
Diseases, 156
Drainage channels, 102
Drip culture, 81
Dry mix, 40
Dry nutrient system, 87

Education, 138
Epsom salts, 31
Excelsior, 59
Experimental units, 56

Ferric salts, 33
Flumes, 11, 114, 116, 131, 135
Food value, 159
Formaldehyde, 120
Formulae, 16, 17, 18
Formulae for beginners, 169
Formula for mixing dry, 170
Foxwells, 130
Fruit jars, 56

Fumigants, 155
Fungoid diseases, 156

Galvanised material, 58
Gases, 155
Gericke, Dr. W. F., 10, 55
Germination tests, 139
Gladioli, 71
Glass wool, 59, 80, 82, 83
Godber, J. W., 89, 128
Granite chippings, 99
Gravel culture, 98
Gravel tests, 79
Gravel types, 109
Gravity feed, 114
Greenhouse units, 57
Guttering, 118

Hardening plants, 48
Heating cables, 120
Hicks, F., 87
Home units, 80, 99
Hormone solution, 96
Hyacinth, 71

Impurities, 23
Insects, 157
Ion exchange, 163
Ionic theory, 42
Iris, 71
Iron salts, 33

Japan, 11, 161

Knop, 9

Laboratory scales, 35
Labour-saving, 11
Leaching, 94
Leaf tests, 148
Leaks, 103
Lettuce, 68, 95

Macro-nutrients, 10
Magnesium salts, 31
Major elements, 10, 17
Manganese salts, 34
Media analysis, 110
Media characteristics, 112
Mercury switch, 105
Micro-nutrients, 10
Minor elements, 17
Mistakes, 150
Mixing line, 135
Molar system, 39
Molecular weights, 23, 172
Motors, Electric, 105
Mullard, S. R., 123

Nitrates test, 147
Nitrogen/potassium balance, 20
Nitrogen salts, 30
Nutrigen, 41

Onions, 67
Osmotic pressure, 48
Outdoor units, 84
Overhead feeding, 85
Oxygen, 61

pH, 42
Paint, 58
Parsnips, 97
Parts per million, 22
Peas, 69
Peat, 59
Pests, 156
Phosphate level, 46
Phosphorous salts, 31
Phosphorous test, 76, 146
Pipes, 86, 119

Plant beds, 59
Plant support, 60
Potassium salts, 30
Potatoes, 66
Primulas, 83
Propagation, 159
Pumice, 99, 109
Pumping, 106
Pumps, 103, 104, 119

Rain, 157
Ratio of elements, 21
Reagents, 50
Rice hulls, 59
Richmond, J., 125
Root diseases, 156
Root removal, 158

Sachs, 9
Salts, 29
Sand culture, 73
Sand test, 75
Sand types, 74
Sawdust, 59
Scales, 35
Seed germination, 59, 91, 138
Seed germination in gravel, 119
Silica sand, 74
Sodium build-up, 151
Solutions
  calculation, 22
  changing, 62, 109
  guide, 171
  making up, 35
  management, 42
  mixing, 36
  stock, 38
  testing, 50
  theory of, 16
  warming, 64, 120
Sparkes, A. G., 131
Spearmint, 9
Sterilisation, 120
Strawberries, 69
Sub-irrigated sand, 89
Succulents, 72
Sweet peas, 43, 130
Switches, 105
Syphon system, 81

Tanks, 57, 58, 118
Taste, 158
Temperature of solution, 120
Testing, 50
Time switches, 107
Tissue tests, 146
Tomatoes, 65, 95, 121, 129
Tradescanthus, 83
Transplanting, 91
Turnips, 66

Units, Home, 80
U.S. units, 11, 161

Valves, 105
Vermiculite, 99, 109

W.P. formula, 169
Warming solutions, 64, 120
Water, 12
Water additions, 47
Water culture, 55
Wick pots, 82
Wind, 157
Wire, 58
Woodward, John, 9

Zinc sulphate, 34
Zinnias, 130